THE THIRD DRAWER

THE THIRD DRAWER

ROBERT W GREEN

ARCHWAY PUBLISHING

Archway Publishing books may be ordered
through booksellers or by contacting:

Archway Publishing
1663 Liberty Drive
Bloomington, IN 47403
www.archwaypublishing.com
844-669-3957

ISBN: 978-1-6657-3339-7 (sc)
ISBN: 978-1-6657-3338-0 (hc)
ISBN: 978-1-6657-3340-3 (e)

Library of Congress Control Number: 2022920974

Print information available on the last page.

Archway Publishing rev. date: 3/16/2023

CONTENTS

FOREWORD

My name is Beth. I met Bob in 2012 and we were married in 2018. We have had over 10 years of a wonderful life together. This book is entitled 'The Third Drawer" and it derives from our kitchen. As Bob is the main cook here, I rarely stray too far from our dining table but one day last year, I was looking for something and I happened to open the third drawer, next to the Viking stove. Inside, I found it stuffed with a bundle of papers containing poems and musings - some typed on an old Royal manual typewriter, others handwritten on everything from beer mats, table napkins and backs of envelopes. I took it upon myself to put them into some sort of collective order. And here they are. I think they tell a story that should be shared. A story of Bob's creative mind and a slice of history over sixty turbulent and emotional years. For the record and in case it's not clear, I love this man - as do many others.

POST 1960

TWENTY-FIVE

I am twenty-five minutes old.
There is blood around my ears
and the side of my neck.
The tissue at the crown of my head
is soft, almost fluid.
People peer in,
watch my mind at work.
My curled body
and bruised face,
my tiny fingers and toes
deceive them all.
I am twenty-five minutes old.
Already,
it has started.

POND SQUARE

Out there,
the square is clear.
So little movement.
A cloud interferes,
with a blade of moonlight.
There is
a slight tightening
of windows.
In here,
nothing moves
that can be seen.
Sounds, amplified
by the cold,
live their own life.
A soldierly tap drip,
the resonant breathing
of old furniture.
Isn't this
a calm account?
An iron description

of a secular night.
The flat language
of needs
embedded in objects.
Trees footbound
in asphalt
and my effects,
my locked mouth.
For an icy moment,
let us admit
to a fractured heart;
your thumbnail
mechanically
scoring
a tinsel frost,
the veinless surface
of my mirrored back.
You won't hear this.
So come back;
please come back.

CONSERVATORY

I am a
banded peacock,
and I have
to get out
of here.
Eleven days
to live,
a third
of my life
already gone.
I'm on high alert
for the tiger
buzz wings—
the black and gold,
mad marauders.
I'm already sick
of Jatropha,
milkweed,
and watermelon.
The mating caw
of the pink flamingo.
The conservatory
has doubles
of everything.
Doors, glazing;
curved ceilings -
so escape
will be difficult.
I must find
a floral,
turquoise
short-sleeved
shirt
to attach to.
Hitchhike
on a human
shoulder
to the bars
of Duval Street
and freedom.
One thing
for sure,
I won't need
a tattoo parlor.

POSSESSION 1999

I have bought a row house
mansion
on North Sixth Street.
The number is
nine hundred and
ninety-nine, and
it is all mine.
The endless rooms,
the dark Victorian fixtures,
and the ghosts
of dead women
belong to me.
What shall I do?
Set them free?
Fold away
the brass stirrups
of the gynecological chair
finished in red velvet,
where the portly
Doctor Strittmätter
perched on his stool
and peered
into pink forests?
Perhaps
I will put in air-conditioning
and paint the walls white.
Play seventies punk

at full blast
in the George Washington room,
with Sid Vicious singing
"God Save the Queen—
you know what I mean."
But this is all
fanciful.
In the gloom
of an autumn afternoon,
I will nod
to my old, black neighbor
sat on his porch,
and creep quietly
through the double doors
and sit at a desk
made from oak,
salvaged from
the frigate *Augusta*,
and listen
to a mournful symphony
by Tchaikovsky,
pretending
that a whole century
has passed me by.
Then I'll get a cold one
from the fridge
and turn on the news.

SHOEBOX

You must burn the shoebox.
The little bits of me
you saved for posterity.
You are twenty-one,
what's the use?
Things we might have done,
sun goblins, everyone.
Burn the shoebox;
start a new one.

SCAFFOLD

Am I paying
attention to
what I see?
A cusp
of snow
on an eyebrow;
a tree line
of fir
and spruce;
the shadow of
an animal;
a clumsily
erected
scaffold
and bodies
seen through
binoculars.
This is
happening.
The mute
coupling
and strange
entanglement
of a naked
man and woman
on a mink coat
in a white field
before the trees
rise up
into the hillside.
Why is there
a scaffold?
Is there
a wolf
lurking,
an aneurysm?

SMILE

"Smile though
your heart
is breaking …"
To be
a meteorite.
Alma,
in a long,
Jewish dress,
standing by
a Steinway
is what a star
is made of.
Her chemistry -
an astronomy
of sound
and mirrored
optics.
I saw her
in fifty-two
and loved
the big tits
and dark energy,
the glimpse of
an unshaven
speck of
armpit hair
in a red
strapless.
"For my next song …"
Now,
on the highest

plains of Chile,
we change physics
from Copernicus
and Galileo
to the edge
of universal
revolution.
I'm a comet,
a screaming baby
sucked from
the nursery
of planets;
a Venetian sailor
seeing
enemy ships
before they crest
the lagoon
as Venus
transforms itself
into crescents
and shadows,
circling the sun.
So the evening
brings a new,
jagged moon,
all cratered
and scarred,
and, "although
a tear
may be ever
so near …"

THE DREAM

max quick
learn to swim
in the dark
the log on the river
walk it rubber soled
reach the bank and
finger the soil
on the far side
sharp now
catch a rabbit
kill it skin it
start a fire
stone skewer it
cook it eat it
walk to the well
draw water drink it
use the tin cup
tied with string
to your belly
at the edge
of the meadow
pause
then cross the field
swiftly on all fours
make for the trees
the air thick
with insects
your milky back
blood red no mind
soon it will be dawn
you will not
be on your own
the sound
from the woods
is your dadas
long and longing
he will find you

ROBERT W GREEN

FORT DIX

A cloud
of puffball spores.
Dawn breaks
above the prison walls
and the first blades
of sunlight
hit the trodden earth.
Cries and catcalls
echo from within.
A din of enamel,
keys and a faint meow.
There is a list
but some things
are best not written.
The hidden birth
of a wild kitten.
The size of a fist.

WANTING

I want to live
with my first wife.
I want to remember
that time in my life.
I want to sit
on the stone steps
by the front door,
with the kids
at my feet
at thirty one.
Quernmore.
I want to sleep
under the stars
in a white bivouac.
I want to drive
down PCH,
like Jack Kerouac.
I want to hear
The Searchers
"Needles and Pins"
and that dance number

sung by the Kalin Twins.
I want to abolish
that word "like."
I want to be Steve McQueen
on his motorbike.
I want to bet my last dollar.
I want to be Harvey Keitel
in *Blue Collar*.
I want to be in Waterlow Park
with a headstone and tomb.
I want my kids
to tidy up their room.
I want to swim for Olympic
    gold.
I hope I die before I get old.
I want the taste
of that first lager and lime.
I want to be in a corner
in my prime.
I want to be that ten out of ten.
I want my life all over again.

JANUARY

January. The forced flowers are dead.
Emaciated daffodils, brought on too quick,
bent back to the stem. Each wizened head,
an old man from a first-floor window.

Taking stock, watching the first snow
of winter, settling on pavements,
more positively on quiet cars. I grow
old by the minute. Double glazed

in this isolation ward. I feel a soft death
imminent. Living above a shop does this.
Looking down, biding time. My breath
patterns on the first layer of glass

seem so appropriate. A contained life, a deal.
Is it real? Carpeted, padded, and sat down.
Tomorrow I'll buy some tulips. "Funereal,"
you said. Good, the pure flakes float down;

the world sort of goes around.

SHOE

Here it is.
Behind a glass case,
one solitary,
crumpled shoe.
A baby lump
of pink satin.
On view,
one little girl's
shoe.
Frail,
poignant,
and hopelessly
unaccusing.
There is a number,
59,572.
Say it again.
Fifty-nine thousand,
five hundred and
seventy-two.
That many.
A shoe
stands here,
representing itself.
Just
the one shoe,
and a word
that begins
in a tremble,
blinks,
and out
of something
that is not
quite
a dream
comes this
gurgling,
unrecognizable
scream.

ROBERT W GREEN

HAIRCUT

Unmasking the evening
into eerie clarity,
three swallows
circle and soar
above my roof deck.
The still blue sky
slowly turning mauve,
south to the city;
north to Temple.
Two vapor trails
of distant jets
are white wire
between high pillows
of cirrus.
To my right,
one woman
over-wined and wearied,
is shorn to the neck.
A footslab
of red hair
remains lifeless
on the single chair
of a hairdressers
in darkening Fishtown.

WINDRIFT 2012

To stay alive
by the sea.
Talking
to myself.
I say it's
for the kids,
doing jumps
in the surf;
but even if true,
it is really
for me.
To be part
of the way
those bodies,
seven and
eleven,
clutch my arm
and cling
to my hip
as a slight
riptide

crisscrosses
the southwest,
tracking
a tired
and top-heavy
sun.
Later on
in this black
balcony night,
their breathing -
synchronized
swimming in
a roll-out bed,
swells up big
self-indulgent
tears.
The ocean,
dispassionate
and now
unnervingly calm,
bides its time.

FOR SYLVIA PLATH

The bees in your box are all dead.
The lifeline from which they fed
has been cut. The sinister buzzing
and the bloated bodies muzzling
against the bee box have given way
to silence. I read you every day.
The terrible sadness. You do terrify.
I shiver at what you say, but I
haven't got the words. I am flat,
a pressed leaf in the Bible. That
is that. Did you die to save us too?
Ach, du. You gave back too much: you, you.
Your tenth life, your fast hole through the sky.
Why? We watched you die. Why?
The sea at Nantucket speaks your name;
we could not stand the pain.

1327 AND 1985

In Tuscany, I am feeling my age.
Note the quickening reaction to cold.
To my right, the sun sinks to its knees—
penance to an early winter
and the shape of the land.
On a small mountain,
charred by other fires,
it flattens out the sky's extremities
by humility and repetition.
Poetically to myself I whisper the word, "vespers,"
trying to time each breath into the bone flesh
that wearies its way up one stone step after another.
In church for holy office, I assume my customary place,
within your hearing perhaps, but out of sight; out of grace.

Old and alone, I am still confounded
by the sound of metal upon metal
and the slow soliloquies of my brothers.
Hoods pulled forward against stiffening breeze,
we move away from the sun's rim of blood
into thickening cowls of darkness
and the comfort of compline.
You sense, even after so many years,
that I no longer belong here,
that I have the desire to leave, to go home.
Departures are more dangerous now but
I must make the pilgrimage back to Provence.
To see a son not knowing his father or when he may call.
For the coming close and the going away of it all.

ROBERT W GREEN

1985

Lower levels abound in the grey whiteness of the sky.
Moving through the reservations
of Medcalf, MacTavish, and the Boulevard de Maisonneuve,
I begin my morning run down to the old port—
a daily ritual to think and be alone in my body.
Fancifully, I wonder what moves
these bony, almost prayer-worn, knees
that take me uncomplaining down to the St. Lawrence.
Strange how threatening the sky feels
as I think of the way the world works.
What connects men with men, their history
and these first, flat planks of the Atlantic.
Of separation, of children, of backs pressed against a wall.
Finally, and not before time, the rain lashes Montreal.

MONDRIAN

What did
Mondrian do
in those
first weeks
of May,
when the sun
spiraled
slowly
across Aldgate,
and the hazy
rectangles
of Farringdon?
Standing here
at the brow
of Parliament Hill,
watching
London
stretch and yawn;
the day
slipping
imperceptibly
into gear
as each tiny,
vertical
variation
of light
flattens out
the morning
shadows
in Soho,
Hammersmith,
and all

the way down
the Uxbridge Road.
Did he
disavow
the sloping hill
tumbling
into the lake,
the curving
cluster
of distant
trees,
or the
disorderly
progression
of back garden
fences
leaning
toward the
brick-built
changing rooms
of the old
running track?
And then
the colour!
Did he
shield his eyes
from the gleam?
Sport
steel-framed
shades
to protect
his eyes from

the onslaught
of green?
This young,
defiant,
laughing,
sparkling,
shimmering
green!
This
glistening,
teardrop,
iridescent
Verdiccio
green!
Foolishly
smiling
in my
cross points,
I begin
the quick
spring walk
back across
the heath.
The Prince
of Wales
will soon
be open,
and I have
business
to conduct,
paintings
to contemplate …

ROBERT W GREEN

THE PAINT OF MARK TANSEY

This is the deal I love.
You put on this work,
the paint at home.
You take it off by the pool
bit by bit, in the cool dusk.
One vast screen where there is
red-brown, the first grey
or teal deep breeze
brought down of a storm.
To three my friend
or four leans back,
thoughts in his chair
by the girl's leg and smokes,
one with a long draw
or more noughts my wineglass
mark a box is back lit.
The torch by the sun
throws, as it dips
its light far to the west.
To the night sky in one
where a man of the urns
stands guard; a young thrush
in the cave, its mouth.
She stares, gapes for a kiss
as one waits
in search for a worm
of a truth; but you
that no more do not see
lives this.

FIRST PEEL (THE BRICOLEUR'S DAUGHTER, 1987)

This is the deal.
You put on
the paint.
You take it off,
bit by bit.
One vast screen.
Red-brown
or teal
brought down
to three
or four
thoughts.
By the girl's leg,
one
or more noughts
mark a box.
The lamp
throws
its light
to the night sky
where a man
stands guard
in the cave.
She stares
as one
in search
of a truth
that no more
lives.

SECOND PEEL
(CONVERSATION, 1986)

I love
this work.
At home,
by the pool.
In the cool dusk
where there is
the first grey,
deep breeze
of a storm.
My friend
leans back
in his chair
and smokes
with a long draw.
My wine glass
is back lit
by the sun
as it dips
far to the west.
In one
of the urns,
a young thrush;
its mouth
gapes for a kiss,
waits
for a worm;
but you
do not see
this.

PINK STRAW

What you do
is this.
You take PCH
into Malibu,
past Topanga
Canyon,
heading north
till you see
a sign
that says
"Geoffrey's."
Then you do
a U-turn
and come back
oceanside.
A blond-
streaked boy
parks the car.
A lookalike
in spick'n span
whites
writes your order
for fresh fish
and sun-dried
tomatoes.
You sit
in the middle
of the day,
sipping ice-cold
chardonnay.
The woman
with you,
by the way,
is wide-mouthed
and voluptuous.
The hand-holding,
the Virgin Mary
between her
soft breasts,

tilts
the pink straw
toward the tip
of her tongue.
You know that
everything
you say
is a cliché,
but you are here.
The California
blue below you
is alive with
sea sparklers.
The mandolin wind
is strumming.
A lady
weightlifter
runs across
the strand.
The surf
has a special
swoosh
as it sweeps
into the shore.
For you,
it is all
flawless.
Sunshine
diamonds
and primary
colours.
You have the luck
to live within
a play,
but your
nonchalant
heart
just ticktocks
away.

TOUR DE FRANCE

The ant peloton
bears down on
an advanced party
of breakaway crumbs,
absorbing them
into its helmeted mass,
and moves on
to a rising climb
of the breadboard
and the flat plains
of granite.
I sit stationary
in my kitchen,
summer all over me.
The Tour de France
on TV, volume down,
so I hear only
the metronome
of my heart,
pedaling mindlessly
at the back of the pack.

GLENN NGEALT

Glenn Ngealt, they call it.
I come here often, drawn by their stories;
the sudden loop of the road that startles the eye.
The blood brown of the bog, its damp yellows
and bleak stacks of compounded graves
mark the end of the ridge
where the black mass of the Slieve Mish
gives way to the sea.

Then the reverse "S" from South East to North West
to stand at its head.
Glenn Ngealt, valley of the mad.
Its inbred cress and low stone walls
maze in on one another,
then escape through harboring fields
into Castlegregory
and the hard green shimmer of the sea.

Dusk sulks in from the bog
narrowing the daylight across the bay.
There is a rustle of cold grass
sheep huddle in the scarp cracks
and I hear it again—
a cry of strangling somewhere below.
A long, frantic echo
scaling the valley wall
and then a final whimper into the sea.
I cannot comprehend, even now,
what it wants with me.

But the drone of the surf;
a sameness of pitch and sound
still surrounds
each lonely farm and shed
and continues.

IN MY CONVERTIBLE

in my convertible
exultant I ride
like a lean man
on a tall horse
i see
sunshine trees
frost jaws
of the morning
spoor of the fox
an imprint
i make no tracks
the empty roads
whistle in
my secretive
mirrors
the carcass
of dead fields
withered snowdrops
my only confederates
i fly
like a lunatic
into the
apple green
sunlight
of the south
for spring
ding a ling
the final
ambush

POEM FOR SARAH

What remains.
Whose
belongings.
Where are
the question marks?
The semi-circular road
that straightens out.
The mysterious dot
in unmarked snow.
Look,
here is the black
Mackintosh chair,
its ladders
pointing up
to a print
of a sheldrake
framed in leather.
Remember -
"red leather
yellow leather,"
and gurgling
at tongue twisters?
Now, here you are,
sorting things out.
Sit down
for a moment.
Hold my hand.

ROBERT W GREEN

DEAD DOGS

Life
and horror
are all
that we have.
When you
were young,
by your own
admission,
you were
an old whore,
living off
old men.
Fearless,
gold fingered
Greeks
or fidgety,
English
aristocrats.
How pretty
the homely
chubbiness
of your cheeks
and that sense
of destiny.
And now
Cockney queens
who know
just about
everything

but nothing
about
the weight
of paint
on canvas
and the way
oil works.
There should be
a preface,
a preparation
for breathing.
An acceptance
of a head
on a wash basin
vomiting
colours.
It is almost
a cold
calculation
of the odds
so your
pope screams
Velasquez
from a triangle
of blood;
but the truth is
you don't really
know
do you love?

THE WATCH

The watch wears
uneasily
on my left wrist.
Its dial
faces inward,
toward my body.
Its movement
parallel
with my pulse,
I watch it.
It waits for me.
I see
the blue veins
struggling
to wriggle free.
A lethal arrow,
a second hand
blood letting
our conglomerate
life.

ORDNANCE SURVEY

On this block,
on this plan,
a baby is born,
and a granny dies.
Think nothing.
For these things
there is no key.
The Ordnance Survey
tells us the pub
the post office and
the disused pump.
Rightly,
these things
are eternal.
People make maps,
engineer symbols,
construct events.
We return
uncharted,
keyless;
crying
blotchy tears
on the edge
of a place.

CROW

An Ogham stone and quern
face my green sea.
The wild fuchsia, the fern

and eucalyptus tree
recall your sad face.
Remember it better than me.

Alone on a stone terrace
the white houses of Cromane
sparkle in the place

of sun shining on corn.
An early morning blue
begins to settle in the forlorn

reeks. A long day begins without you.
A crow on the telegraph wire
flaps blackly into a drying dew.

THE MAN

My thick fist is not clean.
Just empty.
The penny piece is spinning through the air,
catching the July sunshine.
No reflections
except a boy might find it
next harvest.
It was the one and sixpence
that done it.
That was special.
Then there was the missus ten shilling
and the three and a penny rent.
Fourpence union dues
left one penny.
I'd rather nothing
than that.
For this farm
with this body.
For one week
in these long, flat fields,
a final penny.
I'd rather be
the earth itself.
Part of it,
same as it's
taken part of me.
Tomorrow
I said I'd walk to Newmarket.
See if I can get work
with horses.

ANTHRACITE

My father left the farm
in 1908, walked
eight hundred miles to Bremen.
That took over a month.
He waited two days in a camp
by the harbor, for a boat -
a steamship called *Hamburg*.
He had three suits; one on top
of another, some dried fruit
in a bag, a suitcase
and his mother's silver cross.
The trip took ten days.
Far below deck, it was hot,
with much sickness.
In the Great hall at Ellis Island,
he was processed. He had
a few phrases of English,
a name tab (the first syllable mis-spelt),
and a train ticket to Scranton.
It is now a new century
and I am almost one hundred
years old. I remember my mother
made birch beer, Kielbasa,
and pickled beets. I have been
a rich man for most of my life.
My great-grandchildren
know little of this.
They lock their doors,
have elaborate alarm systems;
do not know the songs
in my head; the nearness
of neighbors at night. The smell
of newly mined coal;
the holiness of anthracite.

ROBERT W GREEN

ROSE HARRIET

A black poem expands.
The contusion spreads
into the night; its skin
reaching, overtaking him.
For a minute he stands
and waits. Their heads
strain upwards, pulling him
down. As he wells up and dives
the blobs turn into lives
and the faces begin to break in.

I close the door
and stand there,
allowing the wild night
to surround me; I might
stay here forever. Your
memory lashes in. Nowhere
left now; just your warm light
left to my children and to me.
The rain crashes through our tree.
A great sadness is at my door tonight.

THE MAGIC DRAGON

At evening
in my cave
the sea sounds haunt me.
The rush of pebbles
and demented gulls.
Even now
I still hear your voice.
Deep in my stone walls
I contemplate the damp
and life without you.
The lights bend and glitter
on the far shoreline.
I know you are there.
You are everywhere,
I am the Magic Dragon.
I cried out for love.
You deserted me.
Me and the sea.

EASTER LILIES

Lost in the body of the Mass,
a biological stranger,
surrounded by women and freckled children.

"For the Memory of Elizabeth Lack."
A single, stained glass window, an April sun.
The men stand at the back,

coughing, shuffling their feet.
Grizzled Kerry heads in Sunday bests.
Disjointed fingers, uneven sods of peat.

From stone fields that lean into the sea
come these gnarled celebrants of the cross.
"Today Cccchrist is rrrisen in thee."

The young curate stutters up the hills
of the Easter liturgy and the pope's solemn message for peace.
The communion queue stretches past the few daffodils

of the sparse altar. Mountain sheep brought down
for lambing graze quietly in the next field, ignoring
the arrival of a newish Ford, a mud-splattered brown.

Parked by the lych-gate, the two men from afar
—in well-cut suits—remove a tray of paper lilies
from the trunk of their car.

Blessed and forgiven, we spill out and wait
in the cool sunlight. The men, still separate, gather
by the wall, murmuring about feedstuffs and the creamery rate.

The strangers seem pleasant but say little; nineteen sixteen
blurs into a habit of coins dropped in a wooden box,
and then they are gone. To Castlemaine or Cahirciveen,

they tour each parish on Easter Sunday,
collecting money for provisional arms.
The villagers, now with lapels, go in peace to their farms.

ROBERT W GREEN

THE RAILS

the
rails
diesel
the
relent
less
sound
han ran ratty,
han hang ratty,
hang hanratty

LONDON

London. The distance
was already set
in the telescope
of when we met.
It went back
even further
to the water tanks
of the war.
Balanced on the edge,
our bony knees
reflected like
winter trees.
"Bloodsuckers,"
we called them;
little buggers
that made you itch.
Planning another betrayal,
I think of you
more than usual.
Watching daylight
rise above the Franklin
in a city where once
we made love in.
The blue bridge
throws two loops of light
across the sky.
It is a late flight
out of Heathrow,
arriving at one.
I stand in the shadow
of a pale sun,
knowing
with some precision
the spiderweb
of each decision.

ROBERT W GREEN

ALBERT

Your forlorn face hangs from the bus stop.
Caught in the opposite traffic, I cannot stop.
I feel your unhappiness stretch out to me.
You will be going over Hampstead before tea.

I drive past and this is how we are.
You wouldn't let me drive you in the car.
You are my father, why are we in a wilderness?
I want to be close to you; express my tenderness.

When I see you tomorrow night, what shall I say?
It will be almost two years to the day.
This Sunday when you go for your long walk,
take my children with you and talk.

GOING HOME

The sun slips over
Pacific Coast Highway.
The Palisade palms
bend into the shadows
of Ocean Drive,
and California curls once more
into its wave-skirmished retreat
of happy hours, cocktails,
and sad, unrepeatable bargains.

I drive solitarily
down Wilshire,
stopping to buy baby-
pink roses at Pattersons,
provisions from Vons, and then
turning like a local
into a pock-marked alley behind 11th,
I press my button in advance
for the soothing sweep of the black garage.

It is quietly dark
in the unmade bedroom.
Sick and listless,
you half-doze disconsolately
in the distance of the closet mirror.
"I'll put the flowers in water."
Your lips unpuckered from a greeting peck
slant slowly toward the floor.
Your gaze pursues me wearily through the door.

GENE KELLY

The insistence
of the rain
splintering
into a mist
of not seeing;
the dum, dum
downbeat of
its arrythmic heart.
The start and stop
of each drop,
pulsing and
impatiently waiting
for the swish
of the side foot
flat in the gutter.
I feel you
on my face,
restless
and
relentless;
rain on the brain
and knowing nothing
other than
I want to do it.
To emulate not

the mesmeric
mastery of these
movements between
green lampposts
but to be part
of that pure
expressive joy
and the possibility,
preposterously,
that we will
be set free
through the rain.
That we will see
at the end
of the alley when
the knowing cop
has wearied home
to where maybe
the hint—
or better still—
a tiny glint
of sunlight
beckons us on.
Curb splashing gloriously
into tomorrow.

MORNING MIRACLE

I am trapped.
No, "trapped" is not quite right.
More "contained"
in a rectangular structure
of white plastic,
with compartments
and a mirror on one side.
Poised a few inches
above my body,
just space enough
to be flat
on my back
and make out the lines
that surround me.
Sorry. I almost forgot—
there is a clockface too.
Looking directly down at me,
its glass blurred sufficiently
for the hands
to be unintelligible
and there is no noise.
I have to change
this elevation or
I know I will begin again
those silly hallucinations
that have followed me
since pill time.

My finger finds
the bed button,
and I push it,
hoping for the best.
The head section
slowly starts to rise,
my upper body with it,
and like a seventies
science fiction film,
my containment
slots perfectly
into the facing wall.
I am in my room,
sitting up,
seeing the first sponge
of grey daylight
wash the room
and drip through
the balletic,
blue freesias
into the carded sill.
Against this almost
morning monochrome,
the colour of my
disheveled blood
is really quite heartening,
quite a thrill.

ROBERT W GREEN

KISSING GOD

She has the script now,
fluttering in her fingers.
The sense suddenly
of something there;
the knowledge of
the calm to come
brings a stomachy smile
to the crease of her lips.
The payment seems as unreal
as the daylight.
Notes of that value
do not belong
in a room
so stripped down
to the final essentials—
a mattress, a blanket,
and the sink
so obstinately solid
under the dormer window.

Everything else has gone,
even her door to the landing.
Now the man, too,
three stories below,
closes the Victorian
front door
and is also gone.
Start with the room
and the space where the door was.
Now the door
to where the street still is.
The man walking neatly away,
his brittleness chinking
the glassy morning.
The young woman,
with the scrap of paper
and the hidden paraphernalia.
A sparrow with a worm,
birdsong.

THURSDAY

Took a Boston whaler
around Mountain Point,
past Spanish Town,
and tied up
at the mouth of Devils Bay.
Swam with
the squirrel fish,
sergeant majors,
blue heads,
and baby barracudas
around the reef.
Then clambered
onto the beach
and explored the baths.
Massive
volcanic boulders,
incredible grottos,
and indoor pools
cool and dark,
broken up with
perpendicular columns
of sunlight.
A cross between
a palace built
for Fred Flintstone
and the home
of the Mountain Kings.
Back on the boat,
stopped off at Georgio's
outdoor Italian
bar and restaurant
on Mango Bay
for a cold Corona
before lunch.
Life is hard.

PHILADELPHIA

When the rain came,
it meant it.
At that moment,
the salamander
stood stock still.
There was
a slight darkening
of the glass.
Eleven days
of brute city heat
had taken their toll.
We were waiting
like refugees;
spirits
almost broken,
hanging on
to any quiver
in the yellowing
air
and then
it was upon us -
steaming in
from Missouri,
swelling
its full, fat belly
on the parched streets
of Philadelphia.
It took our
withered roots
and spat them back
in white globs
of rising mucus
so that
our very wetness
became some smokey
indecipherable fire.
The lizard,
streaked in red
and shiny gold,
understood
before we did.
Male or female
it had changed -
and we had
not noticed
that sinuous
transformation.
Anticipating
another potential

and predictable
ending of its
place in things,
pads were grown,
and its behavior
became graced
with some new
and special
knowledge.
The way
its tongue
flashed forward
with confidence
while its tail
had an acquired
but surreptitious
shimmer.
Meanwhile,
we made love
with incessant
and comforting
banality.
I had the thought
that it was not
really our fault.
Perhaps
we had waited
too long
for our papers,
for the country
of our forced
adoption
to take us in.
Never mind.
We are beginning
to learn;
like children
caught
in a storm,
we hold on
to twigs
in a
swollen stream.
Our salamander
advances
while we fish
from a pitched roof
and prolong
the dream.

TWO PHOTOGRAPHS

This is my
retrospective.
A journey
starting with
a photograph
in a backyard.
Short grey
trousers
and nothing else
but braces over
bare shoulders.
A tin bath
in the background,
hanging on a nail
from the door
of the outside lav.
Fast forward
the rest
to just one more.
This time
in colour.
Only
a few years back
at the exclusive
Pyramid Club
in Philadelphia.
Nelson Mandela
and me

sharing a joke,
laughing at
Lord knows what
through the
cigar smoke,
brandy haze,
reminiscing
perhaps
of the good ol' days
and I see
the tracks
made by a truck
out of Pretoria
and I know
there are
no roads but
a series
of interlocking
semi circular
prisons and
avenues where
the end is
the front;
the beginning -
the back
and we wind up
in this god forsaken
cul de sac.

ROBERT W GREEN

THE PRIZE

yes
that
was the prize
the geese
are still flying
the motors swing to a stop
we bowl out
dirty
gasping
for a pint
swearing
the glass
will never touch
our lips
looking back
perhaps that
was the prize
who cares
anyway
the geese
are still flying
they
never stop

IRELAND

Stand alone on the strand
and cast back to strange things
before the Normans, the Spanish,
and the old Irish kings.
Before Ith and the Giodels
arrived in Kenmare,
before the sons of Tuireann
and Morrigan so fair,
before Nemed and the bog men
and their great stone walls,
before Parthelow, the Greek
and the Fomorian calls.
Before Bith and Cessair,
unwilling to pray,
came disowned by Noah
to Ballinskellig's Bay.

Fear not of Tonn Toime,
so deep and so grey
as he roars between Inch
and the edge of Rossbeigh.
We were the people
of this wild mountain land
before the saintly Patrick
and the invaders cold hand.
We lived with the earth
and the clear hillside stream,
we slept with our dogs
too tired to dream.
We worked the steep fields,
just one by one.
we climbed Knockmore
and gave stones to the sun.

Our place was these sand hills
in the long days of light;
when we swam and foot fished,
then coddled at night;
and when the gorse went brown
and the sun solstice died,
we moved into the caves
in Caherconree's side.
When we hunted the elk
and the tusks of the boar,
when we made music from skins
and drank ourselves raw,
when winter filled our rivers
and white flecked our sea;
when rain soaked our soil
til Spring made us free.

And now we build bungalows
and live off the dole.
The state is our savior,
the church is our soul.
Simpletons cut silage
and rent video flicks.
Sharp daughters cook pork
with cheap stuffing mix.
The wards of depression
are full of our youth;
lone farmers with tractors
have forgotten the truth.
Fear and frustration
are the habits now worn.
Our priests and our sisters,
Mother Ireland forlorn.

SAYING GOOD NIGHT
TO A YOUNG LADY

It is as I predicted.
Irrespective of circumstance,
morning comes.
From this dreary hotel window,
I see myself
in the windblown park.
A few gulls wander aimlessly
across empty football pitches.
I think of last night,
finally alone,
trying to sleep, to conjure up your face.
To see it
as I had seen it before.
Happy, tranquil, cross,
I didn't really care.
Laughing, crying,
it did not matter
as long as you were there.
But all I could see
was your shadow behind the glass door.
All I could feel was your hair upon my skin.
I kept hearing the click of the car door
when you left.
A strange mirage of places and smells—
snowdrops, Newmarket, Le Sortilege.
You would think
I would know by now
that this is the way things are.
To part under a cold January star
when our times together
were so warm and far away.
I'm glad anyway.
Our policeman didn't know why
I wasn't saying good night to a young lady,
just goodbye.

THE MIRROR

I am disturbed by strange thoughts.
The flat is more deserted with me in it.
I am standing here
in front of the bathroom mirror
trying to add people to the space.
The mirror worn grey
by familiarities
throws back the same old face.

WEDNESDAY,
SEPTEMBER 19, 2001

Music is
the only way,
not singing -
nothing
with words;
nothing
that attempts
to articulate
what we
are unable
to say.
Far better
the distant
refrain of
woodwinds,
some quiet
oboe in
the pavement
or the cold
clarity of
the French horn.

It does not
matter if
it's a long,
willowy note
by Miles
or a rhapsody
by Brahms
as long
as we can
clutch at
the sound
floating
on air and
understand
the infinite
sad strength
in the final
swoop
of those
death defying
violins.

RENA

Yes, it's winter.
Crisscrossing
the forecourt
at Twenty Fourth
and Aspen,
lost leaves
search for
dead relatives
at the Vietnam
Memorial.
I drive by
your door -
pink and
shivery;
a bare-armed
girl in the
December dusk.

Then, it was
the start
of summer.
Bright sunlight
on the roofs
of Montereggioni;
the drive into
Castellini,
and lunch
in the square.
On the road
to Radda,
I spied
a silver thread
in the haunting
swish of your
long black hair.

KRISTALLNACHT

The sky shows
no remorse.
Carefree, whimsical,
one minute.
Severe, unforgiving
the next.
It's barely morning,
and I'm stepping out
into a breaking
sunlight
of early November.
Reminders
of last night's storm,
little glints
in the stone
sparkle wrongly
like fireworks
at dawn.
Sophie
and Dan
are still asleep.
We all hid
in the back bedroom
above the shop,
praying for quiet.
Sharp and unswept,

shards of glass
mark the contours
of pavement and
its splashes
of paint.
There is
a neutral sky,
stretching
beyond Berlin
and the burning
synagogues.
I breathe the air
but fear
the worst.
I hasten upstairs
to wake
the children,
make urgent plans
for their deliverance
and how to say
goodbye.
Stupidly,
I have one thought.
Not to wear
my father's
long ermine coat.

ROBERT W GREEN

JEVITY

The visiting district nurse taught her
the use of can, syringe, and bottled water.
I've cracked the bastard, she thinks,
the routine of Dixie cup, tube, and sinks.

That's what he said, the husband—frail,
elbow boned but watchful still.
"Cracked the bastard," but he meant more
than the palaver of a bedtime chore.

It echoes around her head and house,
legally assigned, "just in case."
No freedom yet from cloudless nights,
just a starburst of electrolytes.

HOKKAIDO

Instinctively
I check the drop;
a grey lake,
frozen blue
in the moonlight,
and prepare for home.
An east by northeast
scutters the line
between land
and a marble mosaic
of ice.
I start our descent
with a low pitched sound
taken up
through the ranks
till it becomes
a bugle call
of weary relief.
Within minutes
the squadron is settled,
no longer in
flying formation
but a gaggle

of random fatigue.
Here in Hokkaido,
ready for the night,
I look around
the soft white mounds
dusted in snow
and feel content.
For now
the troops are safe,
winding their way
into the deep sleep
of travelers.
My eyes take in
the black tip
of my beak,
sparkling with a series
of perfect crystals.
Without thinking,
I curl it carefully
into the down
of my back
and wait
for morning.

ROBERT W GREEN

THREE

Consider
Houdini's
syllabic
epitaph—
"Magician;
creator;
alchemist."
Oxygen-
deprived,
technical
mastery
finally
defeated.
Deceptor
DOA.

AT THE AQUARIUM

I am
the brown eyed
blue banded goby
patrolling
my grizzled
grey-green rock face.

From crustacean backs
and crevice cracks
you appear
peach-necked
and lustrous;
bedecked in lace.

Shimmering
in your pink
and purple
hydrocoral,
parading your
orange puffball grace.

And then those
sand and
strawberry
anemones,
colourful and black
within the same face!

I could not resist
your open sponges;
your tendrils of coal.
I came
too close,
you devoured me whole.

U.2. 1961

At the station,
Paper stands scrawl
Unbelievable threats
Across our five o'clock
Metropolis.

Expressions
Seep into the
Long escalator
As faces lock,
Harden;

Fade away …

SAN FRANCISCO

Up Divisadero
with Hitchcock.
The boy
disappearing
in the rearview
mirror.
Kids
in the back seat,
tiny cut torments
developing into tears.
In August,
a clear blue
terror.
Life
rising
and falling.
Days in pure
pursuit of days.
The Iraqi
cab man
smiling,
talking
of a poor
sister
in Baghdad
and a previous
fare,
the general to
the Presidio.
At the hotel,
I shepherd
S and M
through the vast
lobby.
"Lubby,"
in recorded
elevator speak.
Airline crews—
BA, Alaska—
form a
nonchalant
line.
In the room,
I turn on
The Olympics.
London,
the city of
an upbringing.
They're showing
black-and-white
shots. Footage
from the blitz.
The never-
ending bombs
and fire.
Then
the cut
to a new flame,
burning
in the glow
of a thousand
faces,
a generation
of new
remembrances ...

THE ROAD TO ANASCAUL

Over the mountain
in the valley
of the beautifully
bewildered
where the iron boned
women
wash and dry
watercress,
grown wild
for a hundred
years or more
and then and now
their hair blown
by the Atlantic,
in slats of sunlight,
across brows
wide enough
to absorb
the patterns of
salt spray thrown

beyond the edge
of the reeks
and again
the men
come in from Keel
and Castlemaine.
Big men,
worn down
by the bogs,
bent fields
and unyielding tides
who don't turn
in their slumber
nor hear
the murmured warning
of the second child
adrift
at two o'clock
in the starless
November morning.

2002

Mr. President, excuse me
talking about terrorists, see.
No sign of a turban or beard
or otherwise no actin' weird.
But they burnt black family shacks
dressed in white and hunted in packs.
Said that queers don't have souls,
Stopped 'em on buses, stopped 'em at polls.
Shot miners digging for a wage;
tore up railroads in a rage.
Made a Midas outa gasoline;
burnt down anything looking green.
Lied about guns, drugs, and nicotine.
So wave the flag, start the parades,
let a million Africans die of AIDS.
Make corporations pay their dues;
it just won't make the nightly news.

GREENBEAM

You said "speak to the bird - he's on my shoulder."
Over the phone, each dumb word made me seem
sillier, older. A prisoner, a tired lag - making noises
now – "hold her closer to the phone." I sag into the
chair. "It's a he," you say. God, put a bag over my
head. A squawking plea comes crackling down the
line. What the fuck is happening to me? Talking
to a bird in peak time on my Star Tac straight into
LA. "He kissed you." "Yeh right, it's beak time."
"That was a joke," I start to say, but you're putting
the bird back in the house. We're in a play of two
characters. You, me, each word is set in the geographical
distance of our lives. Emotions deferred until a particular
instance of some blurred airport out west, where your
eyes find mine. The resistance evaporates. That's
what we do best, I suppose. Create currents of air.
The budgerigar, with wires for its nest and tightly
clipped wings, cannot fly. There is a connection, and
that is the age. The male flaps helplessly in his grey
metal cage.

NORTH STAR BAR/
MICHAEL KROLL

The rub of
eucalyptus
between my
forefinger
and thumb
reminds me
suddenly
of Ballinagroun.
The grove
of baby trees
in late
February.
The daffodils
and death wish
crocuses
yapping
at the heels
of ghostly trunks.
The wind
coming in
from the west,
and cormorants
riding the
sea surf
up the bohreen.
The iris
and wild
hyacinth
swaying
in the swell.
Sing the blues
Michael,
sing.

ROBERT W GREEN

AUNTIE LOUIE

Did you know that this year I'm eighty-three?
I don't say that for you to feel sorry for me.
It's just that it's been such a long time. We
met almost fifty years ago, you see. Yes, that's
how long I've known him. I hadn't heard, you see…
not a word. We used to meet occasionally
for tea. Never ever arranged, but at least we
met every other Saturday. The east stand
at Highbury for the home games. Once when we
won the double, he came to the bar with me
and we drank vintage Moët so majestically
that I thought it was just so wonderful
how he handled everything. His sick wife, she
was in pain for much of the time. The irony
of it was that the painful part of me
that loved him so dearly was his caring
for someone I never met. I phoned the number he
gave me a long time ago. It was probably
the daughter-in-law on the phone. Knowing me,
you know I couldn't say anything except
a total irrelevancy that might establish where he
was. He's dead, you know. I'm so sorry
you already know all that. It's just that Wednesday
was the funeral and I'm feeling slightly down.
The grass at the Clock End has become terribly brown
of late.

CILL AIRNE

What is the conundrum
of the wild rhododendrum;
the riddle of the sea eagle
and the way they mate
within the bracken
of lnnisfallen?
Why puzzle
over a reflection
in the transparent water
of the lake - your face
seven centuries before?
Here is St. Finnian,
the leper,
and the yew tree
of a thousand years.

Here are the stones
of a sanctuary
by the shore
and the kids
clambering up and over
generations of wall.
Herein lies your life
flattening out
almost the last bump
of a mossy plot.
A stepping tread
that may one day
take you back
to the safety of
Cill Airne; or not.

FLO

Does anybody know
what we do?
Flo just got feeble and died.
A camera found her on her side
by the edge of the stream.
Almost tame
at the end.

The background to the bend
in the water was like
a back garden. Like
the way bits of green and a fence
give you the sense
of something else.
People, chimpanzees,

and the possibility
that we see ourselves
in that green stream of sunshine,
sitting mammal still,
waiting for the rains to crack.
Finally, the painful unclambering
from old Flo's back.

MELANIE

The history of a day.
A working grey
convergence;
a production
of tables, children,
and institutional
linoleum.
The smell
of multipurpose
detergent
and the imprint
of infant footsteps
down compulsory
corridors.
Near the end,
by the study door,
a green baize
notice board.
A simple
white-faced card
has appeared
for the first time:
"MELANIE
SPOKE A WORD
TODAY."
We walked past;
stopped
walked back,
and took it all in.
Our face ligaments
struggling
to cope
with a six year
celebration.
November,
the sky breaks through.
The roof
has wonderful blue
holes in it.

ROBERT W GREEN

MAX

My one
year old son
is an
American
and they
are coming home
in flags
from Alabama
and Arkansas;
Lewis and
Letitia,
roadside
explosions—
Winston and
Wynona.
Where is their
testimony?
Lieutenant
corporals
from Connecticut
and Carolina,
Jeannie and
George,
jerk them
from your shoulder
like an AK
forty seven,
rattling up
walls of clay,
dissolving
into streets
of dark
maroon
as the desert
closes down
from Baghdad
to Basra.

FINOLA

Things are not the same now that I am alive.
Once, before we met, I was happily dead.
A sea stone in September rain.
Then you came
and held me in the flat of your palm.
You scraped away my moss, cut back the lichen,
and licked me clean.
The mountains and sea are no longer my people.
At Dunquin, Dingle, and Coumeenoole,
I see your face, the crook of your small finger,
and the colour of your eyes.
Your kiss was a life
I did not want but could not stop;
the mineral held tight
within the small of your mouth.
I feel the warmth of your hair hanging around me,
like the haze of Slieve Mish in late summer.
On the empty whiteness of Blasket strand,
a pair of cormorants call your name
and flap westwards into the wind.
Standing here,
I wish you would turn me back to stone,
and let me remain
the taste of salt
on the brow of your tongue.

METRO SECTION

From left to right …
Sweety Lemons, the gran.
Troy Vaughan, the brother.
Sandra Vaughan, the aunt.
A friend and a fan;
No sight of the mother.

Death hasn't dawned on them
in the photo on the front page.
The metro section; recorded forever.
Arms around each other,
linked by an outrage;
but you smile at the lens, whatever.

Aaron is dead. Just sixteen.
A little black rapper
got shot in the head.
At the Christmas dance
he wore a Santa hat.
"What's up, cuz?" the gang guy said.

Aaron saw the blue sneakers.
"I don't bang, man,"
were the last words he said.
At that age you stand there
as cool as you can.
"What's with the red?" the gang guy said.

Then he shot him close up
because that's what you do
when there's nothing left to fear.
Where there's holly and jolly
down in Rowland Heights,
and it's full of seasonal cheer.

THE SECRETARY

Seven months, soft and round as a cow.
It's children's bedroom time,
the two of them both secure at school.
It's getting hard work now.
The late spring sunshine
promises summer. I will, I will.

It finally overwhelms her.
Flopping on the tiny bed,
her lonely sobs quietly surrendered
to the empty house. Just another
day she wishes she were dead.
The Hoover whines away unattended.

The biscuits soften in the drawer.
Crumbs and cellophane, morning tea
seven miles away. He shares a secretary.
She is desirable. Nineteen, no more.
Tonight he has a secret date. Yes, he
has a wife and two kids. He stirs his tea.

MILLIE

You always start
with something.
Some quickening
of the pulse.
The same springtime
breathing and
breeding. The same
feeling in
the spine that says
quite sharply
that you are here.
But there is
an open door,
and the sounds
and memories
of an aunt
with pints of stout;
singing songs
of who you are.
You walk past
some lively bar
and embrace
the thick knowing
of new deaths
drifting round
like high clouds.
If you still could
you would smoke
a cigarette.
Motherless
and fatherless,
finally
you become them.
And the earth has a centre,
is thoughtful
and forgiving.

LA

I am learning
turning right
on red lights
tipping fifteen
per cent and
distributing dollars
to black men
in braid uniforms
who open taxi
doors for me
in Beverly Hills.

I am thinking
that everything
is goddamn OK
and perfectly fine
as long as its
self improvement
and I can eat
at Michaels
in downtown
Santa Monica
on soft-shelled crabs.

I am loving
a lovely girl
who matches
every lone cowboy
brokenhearted
song ever sung

in my sleek
white Camaro,
caning Olympic
Pico and rednecked
corners on Lincoln.

I am living
in a condo
on Eleventh
with a security system,
an automatically
controlled garage,
a big fridge
that pours iced water,
and a fourteen-station TV
that tells me
I am in my prime.

I am dying
sadly in Cedars,
but I want
all you folks
to know
what a real
swell place
this is to
spend your last LA days
in sunlit dollars,
lox, and bagel tears.

ROBERT W GREEN

SANTA BARBARA,
FRIDAY NIGHT

College kids cruise down State Street,
mountain music meowing from
chrome Chevys, mauve-tinted Mustangs.

The colonnaded palms
and crinkled grass of the sidewalk
swish in an early October rustle.

Almost imperceptibly,
the nervy shifts of air belong
entirely to an immense, incalculable sea.

Waiting higher up in town
squats the muscular façade
of the old Franciscan mission.

Now artificially lit,
it hides hats, the moonlight,
and too many mysterious arrivals.

Here then, in the heart of the dream,
we have the sounds of everything.
Teenagers in cars,

the Pacific Ocean air,
and its palm-swaying swell.
The mission and the tolling of its bell.

BEIT-MERY

The morning
is immediate
as gunshot.
A stunning,
glittering blue.
The jasmine
still lingers
from the
previous night,
softening
the sharp scent
of pine
and eucalyptus.
The hills
of Lebanon,
secure
in history,
weave clean
black lines
into the sky.
Down below,
the pockmarked
city—
mainly white,
cream, and ochre—
crowds on to
the promontory
and stumbles

into the sea.
Beirut begins
another day.
A young Syrian
cradles
an automatic
and smokes
feverishly.
Construction
workers
sit roadside,
eating bread
and olives,
and the traffic
grinds toward
its daily
impasse
of dust
and whistles.
At Beit-Mery,
I look
westward across
the Med.
There was a war,
a recent one.
Now there is
a sort of peace,
and day-to-day

living
develops
a pattern.
It will never
be quite
the same,
but then
whatever is?
I must adopt
that course.
Bury the loss.
Compact it
down flat,
so my heart
and each
difficult breath
can quieten
into a more
solemn
demeanor.
Seven a.m.,
at the
Café Mujar
I try a smile.
The first taste
of coffee
is beautifully
bitter.

ROBERT W GREEN

KILLARNEY

The dawn unraveled
the far reeks
and gave us a day.
A new one,
an unwrapped,
uncomplicated gift.
We accepted it
without gratitude.
Took it in our hands,
played with it
for a while,
and then
finally,
broke it.
The dusk came,
collected the pieces,
and made the hills
a different kind of blue.
Now driving together
into the night,
we take comfort
in each other's arms.
Orphans
with too many presents,
too little love,
we make promises
about tomorrow's gift.
A new dawn.
The assumption that another day
will come
upon us
in much the same way.

EXACTLY 8:35 P.M.

Quietly congratulating myself on
an instinctive feel for time
my head comes up
from the confirmation
of the watch face
and collides with
your startled eyes at the door.

Sorry, you were not to know
I eat alone now
on Tuesday nights.
Yes, the same bistro,
the words written, not spoken.
The bulk of a new companion
shuffles uneasily in your shadow.

THE MAZE

The noise
is one
she knows
but still
hates.
Each time
the same
sense of
dread.
The quick
bang, bang,
bang
of tin lids
on stone walls.
The sound of
the chase
is one
that gags
in the dry
glug
of her throat.
And the
two kids
are more still
than she
would wish.

The eyes
of both boys
are their Da's.
A grey tinge
to the blue;
and like him,
their heads
do not move
as they scan
the glass door
to the yard.
She thinks
of him now
in that
damn place
where there
is no air,
and the stench
bites deep.
Joe squats
on a floor
in the Maze.
This
is how
she spends
her days.

FOR CMG, MAY 2001

1

Friday you do your
shopping in Tralee
and then to Harty's
for a light lunch.
Down Denny Street
to the car and back
home to Ballinagroun.
As you described it,
I saw for myself.
At that moment
in mid-stride,
in the cool Kerry sunshine
of an early afternoon
at the beginning of March,
you saw her
in the faint sunlight
of the street—
the black iron railings
and the tall, indecipherable
windows of the town.
Just a glance
to start with,
then a sort of movement
of the head, a nodding
toward you, a look,
a kindness. A sense
of her, Rose Harriet.
Being there, for you.
How nice to think of
my Mum in Ireland,
letting you know

she was around.
In her life, she
never left England.
Hardly left London
except for our
evacuation to Bradford
in the blitz;
then back to Chiswick.
Yorkshire was too cold -
"let the Germans
do their worse."
And, after the war,
the odd summer week
to pick hops in Kent,
cheap B & Bs in
Westcliff or Ramsgate
and then a graduation
to holiday camps
in the fifties.
She liked the fact
that I married you.
As young as we were
and as timeless
as she was,
she understood
the logic
better than we did.
Too much struggling
against the odds,
too much distance,
prodded departures,

ROBERT W GREEN

and death
upon weary death.
She knew that
each spring was precious,
that the rubble
of the terraced houses
up Crouch Hill
where her cousins
were buried
in forty four
was still there
as an accusation.
And wouldn't she
have loved Inch -
the carpet of crocuses
on the drive up
to the main house.
The panorama
of the mountains, the sea
and God's wild greenery
and the loving bustle
of the Fitzes
as we knew them then
with fierce turf fires,
mutton pies
and Irish coffees
solidly laced
with Black Bush.
And how proud
she would have been
of the separateness

of the country house,
the stables, the mews,
the cottage, the library
and the quern stones
in the terraced lawns
overlooking the bay.
But of course
there would be no
obvious recognition
of any attainment -
"self-praise is
no recommendation"-
and when at fourteen
she caught me
looking once too often
in the mirror,
she gave me
some selotape
and told me,
straight faced,
to fix my ears
to my head overnight
as they were sticking out.
And now I think
of all of this
and the importance
of what she said -
"people, places, things.."
was the right
and proper order
with people a long way

out in front.
And together we would
have walked around
Slea Head and Coumeenoole
on the spongy grass
with the sea spray
of the mad Atlantic
making our faces sting
and our hearts pound;
Then stopped in Dingle
for a pint
on the way home
with that drive
through the valley—
Lispole, Anascaul—
and then the high road
over the Slieve Mish
to gaze down
at the waves rolling in
on the strand below.
I just worked it out
that if life and time,
people and countries
had not overgrown
our well worn path
we would have been
together for almost ever.
Imagine that, old girl,
I guess it means
we've known each other
for forty-two years.

or am I hallucinating
and seeing blobs of time
to-ing and fro-ing,
up and down, and further
and further out of control…
But there you are
walking your dogs
over the dunes
and feeling the wind
that whips the surf
and scatters the snipe
over the sloping fields
that lean into the sea.
And I am
wherever I am
walking some streets
you never heard of
between the cross
of Broad and Girard,
skipping the lines
the same way
I used to as a kid
in Trinder, Sparsholt
and Hanley Road,
past the prefabs
and the puzzled look
of Browell, the chemist,
and Mr. Sims, the cobbler,
who fixed the studs
on my Stanley Matthews
boots for nothing.

ELEGY

The silence
of worn stone
encompassing
footsteps
at a half open door.
Long shadows
seep into the reach
of an unadorned altar.
I sense your bare arm
brush against
the sleeve of my shirt.
Glancing
at your face.
I catch four
perfect diamonds—

blue, green,
brown, and gold
follow one another
across the nape
of your neck.
I'm not sure
whether or not
that's a smile
but it goes
a long way back.
To old summers
in Clare
and the way
the hay lingered
longingly in your hair

FRANKFURT

We are
realists.
We are
frightened
of ourselves.
We are
scared
of what
we will
eventually
find out
about
one another.
Who were
our friends,
our neighbors?
What did
they know?
What messages
were taped under
the condom machine
in the café
at Prenzlauer Berg?
What did
we say
about
each other?
Who saw
the shape
of the shadow
creeping
from the room
of Helga Soss
at two
in the morning?
Maybe
even she
was Stasi
and laughs aloud
at our ludicrous
buttocks,
sagging
with beer
and old regrets.

Smiling at the
cross reference
of our reports
and our poetry.
Sanguine
about the victims
and our
universal
treachery.
We are "free" now,
living
in isolation
in Frankfurt.
We no longer
communicate.
We are all
burnt;
our skins
peeled away
by truth
or this new
dimension
of fear.
We shudder
at each archive
opening
and the phone
ringing
before seven
in the morning.
And then
there is life.
The vengeance
of spring,
the sweetness
of intermittent rain,
and the green
shoots
that disdain
buildings
and mock
the permanent
greyness
of our skin.

ROBERT W GREEN

WEDNESDAY,
SEPTEMBER 11, 2001

Today
things are in
the past tense.
I used
to draw them.
The Twin
Towers.
Compulsively
doodling those
clean limbed,
elongated
rectangles.
A quick
horizontal
scribble did
for the floors
and sometimes,
when inclined,
I would fill
in the gaps.
The white
paper space
between
the plaza
and the river
and then place
those biblical
blocks in a
safer home,
by shading in
spires and
the lower
Manhattan
skyline.

Today,
three thousand
people
are dead
or dying,
trapped
and punctured
in this living
TV scrawl
of spikey steel
and twisted
windows.
Whatever
happens now,
we have lost.
Whatever
we do
or say.
Some sense has
disappeared
from the edgy
rays of sun
slicing through
the Avenues
of the world.
Once again
we have
unleashed
upon us
the worst
weaponry
known to us.
It is both
ourselves.

WORDS

Each word
counts
for less.
Every
possession
counts
for nothing.
Hang on
to the little
you know.
Give away
the rest.
Keep
in your heart
the moon
moving across
the heavens.
It is only
the dark space
on the shelf
and the bare
window
in the wall
that gives
the shelf
and the wall
their relevance.
Look at
the stars.
The trapeze
artists
unclipping
their stays,
fingertipping
their switches,
embroidering
the swell
of oceans
with their
midnight
shimmer.
Think
of a time,
a place
and the seamless
indifference
of the universe.
Tugged
by the perpetuity
of tides,
the predictable
logarithms
of love
lose their
sanity
and their place
in the elements.
What is lost
is gained.
What is gained
is the same
sense of loss
and the unknown
knowledge
of another
Greenwich
Mean time
tomorrow.

ROBERT W GREEN

EMPTY GYM, DECEMBER 2007

The first traces of snow.
Don't let go; don't let go.
Five miles on the machine—
the man says you're Bob Green.
Keep up this mad pretense;
live life in the present tense
until the day you finally stop,
arrested by some genetic cop.
Defeat those declining strengths;
this morning start swimming lengths,
juggle the plates,
hit the weights
until your tailor,
like Norman Mailer,
says, "Can't make it fit—
you're full of shit!"
Now an old Chevy will not start;
its brain is cranking, not the heart.
All those zeroes on the clock—
can't you hear that *knock, knock, knock*?
What a fuckin' serious state—
colon, kidney, enlarged prostate.
Don't listen to those doctor cunts;
cars and people wear out at once.
Transmission, tires, brakes, and steering,
shoulders, back, eyesight, hearing.
And all those avid social climbers
deep in the grip of old Alzheimer's.
Homeless blankets over steam
living the great American dream.
And off the treadmill, there you stand,
thinking of the Promised Land.
Sweat dribbling down your bony frame,
no one there to give acclaim.
You walk away, matted hair,
pondering the wear and tear.
And no matter how bad the end,
perhaps it's better to pretend.
Tune out the voice far inside,
and live your life for those who died.

FUNERAL

The road into town
was dead and senseless
until the quiet sedans
slowed to a black crawl,
and pale, freckled girls
slipped out of painted doors
and old-fashioned shop fronts.
Women in dark coats,
joined by old farmers
creased with fieldwork
and their lanky sons
in ill-fitting suits
and sullen ties.
A small procession of cars
became a much longer one
of people moving by the hundreds—
a blur of faces, fingers,
photographs, and rosaries—
until all were assembled
into the vast well
of the old stone church.

ROBERT W GREEN

MENAGERIE

Can you feel their fear,
hear their hearts beat?
Baby white mice,
two to a handful,
dropped face down
into the glass-encased pit.
They stop, twitch,
and shiver for a second.
Then scurry toward
the shadow
of a few sparse rocks.
And the solace
of momentary darkness.
Gliding by
comes a mouth
twice the size
of their being.
At that time,
is there a knowing
in being bred
for death?
The darting tongue
has its own brain
that drills into
a promise, an inevitability.
The pythons
curl up
in fat admiration,
their dry skins
shimmering
in the artificial light
as we look on,
fascinated in our own
apocalyptic bewilderment.

PUTIN THOUGHTS

You let us steal.
We let you live.
What more
should I give?

Now
there are no
citizens,
just subjects.

We have lost
all human feeling
when we measure
the dead
in zeros.

ROBERT W GREEN

HOPE

Hope has no border.
The ambition
of a two-year-old
has no boundary.
Freedom
has no frontier.
Words have no exile.
A train leaves Ukraine.
What was the question?
Can there be poetry
after Auschwitz?
What is the sound
of smoke
evaporating into
the woods,
the morning air?
Poland, Lithuania—
where are they?

Yes, the words
endless, restless,
and let loose—
running over rivers,
slipping into
the Gulf Stream,
hovering high
on the wind.
Hope has no border.
The ambition
of a two-year-old …
Repeat, repeat
after me.
Freedom
has no frontier.
Even on
a headstone,
words have no home.

VIRGINIA TECH

On a swing
in a park
at the end
of April,
when the new
born green
takes your
breath
away
entirely,
he sees her.
In that
yellow dress
that only
a six-year-old
with red hair
and a lace hem
could wear
and laugh
in tune
with the
pointless
repetition
of the sky.
And her legs
one moment
stretched

full tilt
and then
hugged back,
leaning into
the trees.
All this
he sees
as he does
his thumb push.
The number
pre-programmed
into some system
he does not
understand
and the moment
when CNN
reports live
from a place
that registers
from afar -
begins
the continuous,
and forever
unanswered,
ringing
of a distant
star.

SOPHIE AND MAX, 11/24/21

Trembling
with new fissures
and walking
into a room
with a black table
and an over scented
fragrance
of white gardenias;
calmed by
the first glass
of a twenty eighteen
bottle of Meursault
and the thought
of its insignificance
in the scheme
of things.
And deciding
to put this down
on the eve
of Thanksgiving,
without asking
why and what
the hell
does it matter
or even mean?
And you know
the answer—
the hieroglyphs
of our brain.
The happiness
of kids.
The pain …

COVID

In a dream,
words stamped
on my eyelids.
Hooded Merganser,
black crown;
emerald neckskids.
Waking
in the middle
of a lake
around midnight,
my heart
paddles feverishly
to stay afloat.
By my side
the young bride
snores quietly
in her secrecy.
The shore beckons.
A dawn
is reckoning.

AFTER CHRISTMAS

"Not dead"
said Murphy,
"just still."
The wren
again
in a box
given
on the day
of Steven.
The captain
made and
betrayed
by the song
in a hedge
looking over
water in
Fermanagh.
Now we cure
a heap
on the floor,
crumpled
by the cross
of Saint George;
sworded
by a boy
in glasses
and saved

by a girl
with freckles
and a pretend
Doctor's bag.
Sing, sing,
my old
Minehead
children
and dreamers
from Dingle.
Sing, sing
from St. John's
to Philadelphia,
"Oh Joe, Oh Joe,
the boat
is going over"
but hold tight
to the pints
of the black stuff
as we hit
the gangway
and roll
mummerly,
slowly swaying
deeper into the
down of South
Second Street.

HULAGU'S PRAYER

Fuck you,
baby heads,
deliver or die.
Can't you see
that your shiny hair
and good manners
appall me.
My mares
and bow-legged body,
bloated with
blood and milk,
were made
with God's will
to crush
you wriggling worms
beneath the planks
of my Kumis table.
Thank Allah
that serves
to show me

the reflections
of the sun lake
so I sense
my face,
big like
a boar
with black-
granite teeth.
And grants me
the gurgling
ripples
that diminish
your sobs
and grunts
as the mass
of your heads
edges away
from my
beautiful
stench.

THE RAID

A party of
herons raid
the south
shoreline.
Soaring in
from the firs of
Ballinagroun,
they cross
the marsh,
the dunes,
and the
foamy
aftermath of
an early-
evening tide.
Then,
circling wide
of the sunset,
they
approach the
sea from the
dark shadow
of the hill.
In the
reflective
echo of the
strand,
their chill
croak hangs
upon the air:
Kill-kill, kill-
kill,
kill-kill.

J. H.

We ambled single file
into Sheriff's meadow,
down a dense trail
of white pine and spruce.
As the path forked,
the field opened up
and, in a moment,
it became everything.
There was the swan
on the still, blue pond,
the marsh grass,
the ribbon of sand
and the bobbing boats
of Nantucket Sound.
Out of the sea lavender
and honeysuckle
rose a blue jay
and a yellow oriole.
I caught
the widening whiteness
of your eye
as almost imperceptibly,
you gasped.
And then
the only thing
I could see
was your expression
from yesterday,
when frantic with desire,
we had to turn into,
of all places,
Scrubby Neck Lane,
park down a cutout
in that dusty road,
and surround one another
simply and furiously.

ROBERT W GREEN

SOMEWHERE IN EUROPE

There is a glade
in Europe
where in season
there is leaf upon leaf
and the sprinkling
of sunshine.
Forty-eight years ago
a few drawings came out
clamped to the bones
beneath his shirt.
The Americans came in
and burnt the factory
where the rest were hidden.
He spoke in Polish
about one of the pictures
that survived.
It was in charcoal,
black upon grey.
The subtitles
came up on a TV screen
beneath the drawing.
Even without them,
you knew
what he was saying
by the sound
within his voice.
"I saw this pile
of dead and dying …
it was moaning, creaking
shaped like a pyre.
The almost living
were calling and coughing,
shoulders like scalpels.
It was dusk
in January,
and I remember
the snow clouds
gathering in the east.
In the morning,
outside the gates,
the large white mound
was finally quiet;
eventually
and eternally
at peace..."

THE LATE POEMS

Coughing
in the garden chair
at sunset,
waiting for a pill.
Bluffing
my way through care,
unpaid debt,
and sort of being ill.
Hidden rhymes
you cannot see
are read
with resignation.
My "Late Poems"—
the littered debris
of a dead
imagination.

LISTOWEL

Certain things need not be said.
Raindrops glistening
On an April leaf.
The disappearance of mountains
Into the sky.
The sea changing colour
Over a coral reef.
The baby ward echoing
With Sophie's first cry.
These flat platitudes are dead.
They are no more,
Lifeless at
Listowel's grim door.

KAFKA

You and me,
Franz,
This mist.
The fear that stills;
that spreads;
that longs for
a sense of
what is great
or what is small.
That knows
the deep, damp well
of the soul.
Up here
in our gaunt heads
where the blood
of the brain
meets the whites
of the eyes,
we lock up
our tongues.
We are Jew dogs
in Prague.
Our hind legs
stuck in the past,
our front paws
scuff the dirt
as they try

to take some hold
and ease the trap
that bears down
on our backs.
You know
what goes on.
We have both
seen it.
You said that
you were like rock,
like the stone
on your own grave.
At the end
of it all,
it comes down
to them.
Words.
The glint
from a cold sun
on a tin can
at dawn
that lights up
a bare wall.
Your sounds
by Max Brod
break out
from the brick.

ROBERT W GREEN

REVELATIONS

In Moscow,
the sky is at work.
Snow clouds surround
the summer palace.
The tiny rib cage
of a certain
silver headed lady
shudders at the moment
the sky moves,
knowing something.
Her son
drives for a taxi firm
based in Pasadena.
He has a fare to Hollywood.
She edges up the queue
as though it is the thing to do.
To be here, waiting
in a long line
for whatever
and the tension of
the snow not yet falling
and her son slipping
into the Santa Monica freeway.
She reasons fearfully
about this to herself.
She and him
have wanted too much.
The ration runs out.
He picks up a Polish émigré
who has made it good.
Back down the line,
there is the sound
of a kerfuffled shout.
The equation works out.
Eventually everything is equal.

FOR VICTORIA

An image.
The camera
is on long shot.
The day breaks
cold and clear.
A train
carrying cargo
slices through snow.
Its silky trail
underlined
with immaculate
precision.
Cut
to close up
and see my face,
crystals sticking
to a two day beard.
Bits of ice and grey.
A particular way
the wind catches
the spittle diamonds
around my mouth
and spins them
into the mountains.
I am hanging on
for grim death.

Do you know
I am fifty years old
and still see myself
in movies.
Old ones now,
just about
in colour.
I have things to do,
brushwork obligations.
Individual blobs
by Pissarro.
The sky
has an edge
of nectarine.
People
will not believe
this clarity.
The iron
clenched into the teeth.
I jumped freight
in Nebraska,
clinging to
a frozen guardrail.
I cannot let go.
I'm expected
in Kansas.

ROBERT W GREEN

PINBALL

There is
always
this blurring
of the lines.
An un
certainty
as to whether
they were
ever there
in the first
place.
The car
tography
of our ex
istence.
The arcade
of history
is the only
way we can
know who
and what
we are.

And yet,
and yet …
we are all
survivors
of the same
orphanage.
Our lives -
little tilts
on the pinball,
pulsing
between
the flippers,
until
gravity
takes over
and thuds
it clanging
down
into that
eternal
static
silver slot…

THEODICY

The storm
after the stillness.
The knock,
knock, knock
announcing
the return
to ordinary
chaos.
The looming
rumble
of life after
the silent streets
of a state funeral.
The porter
gets on
at Monument,
changes at Moorgate,
and then the black
Northern Line
to Finsbury Park.
The gasp
of tube doors
closing;
the *click, click*
of escalators,
faces reversing
back into
the early chatter
of a lobby
and the first

pavement cigarette
of the day.
We are separate
and together.
Yesterday's
snorting horses
flaring up
in the wind chill,
framed against
chamfrons and
square shouldered
cavalry.
Clip clopping
down the streets
of our ancestors
and dead cousins.
Was there ever
a recording
of our regrets,
our neglects.
And speeches
we didn't make?
Perhaps now
compacted
in a newly mastered
box set or within
the flattened leaves
gleaming
of that golden
fore edged spine.

ON THE TREADMILL

Pushing the green button for a quick start,
the rubber earth revs up to meet my heart
as I move my finger to the arrow for pace
and mentally adjust to its digital face.
I am running along a wide, empty strand
on the barefoot chill of six o'clock sand,
demented gulls, and the sound of the sea;
my toe prints quickly disappear from me.
In the mirror ahead, the whites of Cromane—
cottages and fields, a developing dawn.
Pounding along at my nine point five,
thinking of how we have to survive.
And learn from those who went before
that needed less yet arrived with more.
The reeks and Slieve Mish are my arena
that ignore this ragged, sweaty demeanor
and swallow up skinny legs and arms,
the same way they do with stone-walled farms
and the backbreaking turf cuts in the bogs,
the crack of morning, and the work with dogs.
Now the point looms up and the dunes diminish.
I am exactly halfway from start to finish.
Two and a half miles reads the distance rack.
In my mind, I turn and begin to run back.
With a breeze behind me and the sand turning warm,
I am floating along without feature or form.
The expanse of the Atlantic, grey and immense;
the cormorants wheeling in wild innocence.
Then the hotel and houses come into view.
Above, on the hillside, cream, yellow, and blue.
The gorse and wild fuchsia tumble to the road,

where a horse and cart and their creamery load
make their way home from Castlemain town,
past Bolteens, Lack, and Ballinagroun.
Now the breeze block shop at the turn of the beach
comes steadily closer, but still out of reach
to see an inscription painted on the wall
that my daughter read when she was two feet tall.
The last quarter goes by as my five miles end,
and I kiss the sea air as my two worlds blend.
Then push the stop button and stand on the rim,
sweating and panting—just a face in the gym.
But the weight lifting heavies and big muscle freaks,
veins popping out from their biceps and cheeks,
all they see in the mirror are haunches of meat,
not the green fields of Kerry or the smell of peat.
So I saunter out with my own private grin.
Tomorrow I'll run through the streets of Turin.

ROBERT W GREEN

ATLANTIC CITY

It is around 10:00 p.m.
An upper window,
the Forum Lounge
at Caesars.
Looking down
on the boardwalk.
I am cocooned
in a bar.
A swivel armchair
in soft fabrics
a red carpet, brass
and the heads
of Emperors
etched in glass.
At the piano
a black man
in a white jacket
croons a number
by Billy Eckstine.
Below me
in the warm
and fuzzy air
is a tableau
by Pieter Bruegel.
Blobs

of casino light
cast distorted shadows
on the wooden slats
of the promenade.
The villagers—
men, women
and children
assemble
in a moving
landscape
that constantly changes,
yet at its centre
remains unnervingly
the same.
The pigments
within the sky,
the misty full moon
and the receding
shelves of the ocean
are a background
brown, black
and navy,
with skirmishes
of off-white
where the pier

falls away
into the sea.
Century
into century
come these faithful
replicas
of the night,
the sea and
whatever.
The people
trapped
in this gilded frame
are also
the same.
No longer
in doublets
or pantaloons
but in tee-shirts
and cut-off jeans,
shaking their
plastic beakers
of tin tokens
to hear
those satisfying
clinks of
what it means

to be
in this place
on a Saturday night
in August.
And in all of this
there is a peace.
A comfort
of knowing
that whatever
is sermonized
about a scene
pregnant
with money,
drink and sex,
it is not,
to any extent,
different than
the sense of
movement,
merriment and doom
of the artist's
peasants
obliviously
dancing past
the quiet magpie
on the gallows.

ROBERT W GREEN

FOR EUGENE

The low lament
of a recorded
bugle.
The flag,
triangulated
as some sort
of belated
present.
An open,
four sided tent
in a meadow
where mourners,
like black
swifts,
gather and
flutter.
Water
dribbles around
eight patches
of tarpaulin
into the gullies.
Near
a new mound
of broken earth,
an old rabbi
whispers
in Yiddish
to the family,
sat in the front row.
Magritte
umbrellas
bobbing
in the sky,
people
still arrive,
assembling
in the wet grass.
Now
a slight chill
hangs over
its dampness.
Life

dissolves
like sounds
and phrases
in a stiffening
breeze ...
basement
stationery,
scissors
in a garden;
and the quiet
sobs
of red-eyed boys
remembering
the clambering
over the torso
of a tall man
with long arms.
Their faces
pale in the
grey light
of early
October.
And then
it is over.
The huddled
congregants
disperse into
a perimeter
of parked cars,
start up
engines,
and drive away.
The empty
Cemetery;
a singular
coffin
and the bronze
plaques
glistening
in a glimmer
of orange trying
to break through.

DAN

Sometimes it seems
I'm on stilts,
heavy-legged,
clumsily surveying
the long valley landscape
that slides inevitably
into the sea.
Stumbling to make sense
of that sudden splash
of semicircular blue
as the corner turns
sharply at Lispole,
and I'm still
tottering into
some dull memory
of a single phone call
and the long ringing
that changes
almost everything.

But here are
the white gloves,
stained blood-red
by the wild blackberries
along the bohreen.
Here the school blazer
you wore for the pledge
stiffens in the breeze.
Here the proud watch.
And now lurching
along the straight stretch
of the Dingle road
below the cut
of the old railway,
I hear that smoker's laugh.
One deep and serious chuckle
that can only be you
as you figure out the answer
to yet another desperate clue.

CRYIN'

One time
in Arkansas,
I blacked my face
to get a job.
Jesus!
Can you imagine that?
A paddy
singing and playing
plantation songs
for rednecks
in their jugs?
Not that
I had much time
for blackies mind,
but then
they didn't know
me either.
It was what
smart folks
called parody
but I know better.
Leastways,
they understood cotton;
My Gran Da from
Kilkenny
knew spuds.
I tell you
cryin is
the same place,
makes the same sound.
That's for sure.

SENTENCE

Meanwhile
a sentence stakes out the hill.
She is stuck still.
A word keeps an eye out
for magpies in flight.
Daylight
knows what it's like.
The ache
waiting for a heart to break,
the clouds getting
in the way.
What will the word say
if he stumbles across a dove
instead of a thief;
love instead of grief?
Beware;
The sentence does not move.
Clauses as brittle
as withered roots
await the inevitable crunch
of her camouflaged boots.
So if you must know -
I am scared, unprepared,
and alone.
All I own is them;
Both male and female;
seen and heard;
the sentence, and now
the word.
But they are no
comparison
to your hungry,
disdainful
garrison.

SUNDAY AFTERNOON

A darkening afternoon
sweeps across the plains
of East Anglia.
The flat fields
are on edge.
The occasional tree
shivers with
the predictability
of a nervous sentry.
A series
of communications
crackle across
the ley lines.
Parked in an
empty road,
I wait for you
in the car.
A water tower,
gaunt under
a wheyish sky,
blocks out
your cottage
at the end
of the lane.
When you appear,
scarved and
mackintoshed,
with the excuse
to your husband
yapping at your legs,
not believing his luck,
you say,
"We have five minutes,"
and surround my mouth
with yours, and
I know that
I am in a film
again.
But the thunder
that I hear
is real,
and God
finally
makes contact,
not as a magician,
but as another
perverse electrician.

A NICE WAY OF LOOKING AT IT

On the right side,
my eye is flat
within the surface
of my face,
the socket beyond
worn away
by an ache
that dominates
the sinus membranes
underneath.
A glass coffee table
with a painted iris
is a nice way
of looking at it.

On the left side,
my heart is bent
within the confines
of a day;
the rib cage beyond
broods away
in floods

that resonate
to Sibelius
deep below.
A Finnish abattoir
with a whistling butcher
is a nice way
of looking at it.

In the middle
is a stranger
unable to feel
direction.
Turn him to the right,
and he will
become blind.
Left is the cliff
where he falls in love.
What the fuck?
A snake suddenly still
in a bright mongoose pit
is a nice way
of looking at it.

ROBERT W GREEN

MIDNIGHT JASMINE

Like a bloated mosquito
buzzed out
on my alcoholic blood,
you are belly heavy
with each fat secret.
Languishing
on the ceiling,
you look down
at the pock marked bumps
you have bitten into my face
and the tendons of my neck.
In a dark room in Rome,
previously hidden molecules
at some private alchemy
are sucked into
your transparent funnel
that distills and isolates
the fact that, yes
once I fucked Melissa
or was it Clarissa
or Theresa -
from the time, the place
and what is always
the ultimate sadness
of circumstance and infamy.
Now you bumble about
stumbling down toward me
from that old oak wardrobe,
drunk and luscious
and inevitably doomed
to a magnificent red morning.

THE JOURNEY

Drove
the two eight three
out of Laramie
down to Denver,
Colorado.
The first day
of February,
late eighties.
The big Lincoln
knows this road -
its bonnet
like a liner
in soft swell,
nosing homeward.
My breathing
is easier here.
In the cataract
blue air of slim
Wyoming motels
a double gulp
starts the day.
Now cruising
an hour away
through these
flat, white fields,
the thin
swallowing lump
is still.
The crisscross
randomness
of snow breaks
makes a peaceful
pattern like
the tidy scars
of heart surgery.
To my right
the land sheers
into scenery.
Perfect
cardboard cut-outs
of the Rockies.

Earthman, moonman,
beggarman, thief—
this country
has a fascination
for its version
of the truth.
On Interstate
Twenty-five
I pass a lone trucker
between Wellington
and Fort Collins.
Raising an arm
from a chrome cab
he calls "Hi"
and I know that
I love this place;
it is so
overwhelmingly
American.
My life lies
flattened out
behind me.
All these pressed
flowers
in old books.
And today
the implacability
of mountains.
Alone
and surrounded
by the stuff
of dreams
and highways.
Earth and air;
death and sex.
The aeroplane sign
says next two exits.
Unconnected.
I have
a one-way, single
into LAX.

UNCOUPLED

The narcosis
of love.
Deep diving.
Four minutes
of pure
unbreathing.
The brain
uncoupled.
The you
and the deep blue
I lowered
head first into.
The management
of a pulse
in the darkening
descent.
The last rods
of sunlight,
shooting upward
to a disappearing
surface,
unconcerned.

DECONSTRUCT

A resistance in the distance.
Runes, locks; dunes, rocks.
An inkling, a twinkling
of human rights, of fairy lights.
There, here …
a bare, a clear
fangled glee; green sea,
dogs whooping; fish looping
at the, through the
numbering wave string.
Slap rhythms, flat algorithms
of punishment; of movement
flout further out
fairness, darkness.
The chancing is advancing
in a form with a storm
of rainbow dance, a limbo dance.
A tightening of lightning
marching into; arching into
the rackened, the black and
throat loses purple bruises -
its final cry of the sky.

A resistance.
Runes; locks.
An inkling
of human rights.
There,
a bare
fangled glee.
Dogs whooping
at the
numbering.
Slap rhythms
of punishment
flout
fairness.
The chancing
in a form
of rainbow dance.
A tightening
marching into
the rackened
throat loses
its final cry.

In the distance,
dunes, rocks.
A twinkling
of fairy lights.
Here,
a clear
green sea,
fish looping
through the
wave string.
Flat algorithms
of movement.
Further out,
darkness
is advancing
with a storm.
A limbo dance
of lightning
arching into
the black and
purple bruises
of the sky.

MIX

It's the same old mix
A sign of the cross
The crucifix and
The burden of loss
Goodbye papa
Jeez how I miss that man
You were the guy that always ran
Goodbye papa
Jeez how much I miss that man
It's the same old tale
A sign of the time
This old holy grail
And making words rhyme

COVID-19

They're torching towers
in Birmingham. Here
I'm wearing a white mask
at Whole Foods.
As an old man
they let me in
at seven in the morning,
zipping down the aisles,
chucking stuff
into my wire trolley.
What larks!
Lilies and late tulips.
Asparagus
and sugar snap peas.
The young black man
at the butcher's counter
can't wrap up
a five pound leg of lamb.
My days
as a ten year old
wrapping meat at Dewhursts
in Crouch Hill
every Saturday morning
come careering back.
Raw embarrassment
for the poor guy,
who is blushing
without a tinge
to his skin.
I so much
want to help him,
show him how to do it.
The angle of two sheets
of greaseproof paper,
the crossing over
of the sides,
the quick roll over
and fold.
An old guy

at the back
comes forward
and fixes it.
Winks at me,
and I'm on my way.
Bread, juice, milk,
eggs and cream cheese
are around the next corner.
My son has asked for
creamy peanut butter,
and my daughter wants
fresh all-on bagel.
They are so American;
it makes my eyes
spark and tearful
in that vast coastal shelf.
They are teenagers now
and still sleeping.
Tonight I'll make them
dinner—prosciutto-wrapped
salmon, garlic mash,
baby carrots, and zucchini.
And they have trouble
with toast?
Where—or did I—go wrong?
No, no; they know stuff
I cannot comprehend.
Talking in a language
interspersed with "like"
as strange and novel
as COVID-19
that stretches far beyond
the rivers
we live in between.
The memories are on file.
"So pack up your troubles
in your old kit bag
and smile, boys,
smile."

ANOTHER SIN

When she saw Soutine's
blood flesh raw
hanging on hooks
and the looks
that came my way.
I had to say
it really wasn't me.
I had to put her
out of her misery.
But you don't believe me;
all you see is red roadkill,
and the faintly still-
stuttering heart,
and the start, pause, stamp
of my frozen foot
on the back of her head.
We lay quietly in bed.
Your nightmare about to begin
as each showing begets
another sin.

ROBERT W GREEN

OVERCOAT

In the darkening
dusk of Los
Angeles lost
souls, seemingly
formless, shamble
away from
the center
to make shapes
that become
a pattern as
precise as a
Busby Berkley
movie.
In a musty
overcoat
much too large
for my frame,
torn around
the pockets
and buttonholes,
I am part
of the movement
that creates
this sweet syntax
of despair.
But wait -

if I have
the strength
to lift my
albatross arms
and flap heavily
westward,
I can reach
the sea
before the sun
finally disintegrates
beyond the rickety pier
and allow myself
to hang awkwardly
in the air,
collecting
jewel drops
in my eyes
from the Ferris wheel
and whirligig.
An old pop song
is playing in
the happy-hour pub:
"Sweet dreams
are made
of this, who
am I …"

HOMECOMING

They bring
the bags back
in wide bodied
Boeings.
Draped in flags
of stars
and stripes,
received in
crisp salutes
and sometimes
coordinated
gun fire.
The grocer
and his silent
wife
bent over
in grief.
The still man;
a locked store
in Hope,
Arkansas.

ROBERT W GREEN

TULIPS

Who bothers about
the copper coins
in the base
of the Steuben glass vase
stretching out
the thin stems
of manufactured tulips.
I do.

THE YOUNGEST BOY

Einstein spiraling
corkscrew curls
haloing your head
in a silky red,
the softness
of your cheeks,
and the hazel
wonderment
of your wide-
open eyes
as the dog
next door—
a squat
Rottweiler—
begins its
brazen bark.
Then the
perfect purse
of your lips
and the fearless
double breath
of an unblinking
oof oof.
The world
outside
and what
we have done
go quiet
for that one
moment
of recoil
as the last
reverberated
crackle of
the blast
is stilled,
and our dust
slowly rises up
in the wake
of unrecorded
smiles
and sorrow.

ROBERT W GREEN

THE MAYOR'S ENTREATY

Last weekend I went to New York,
harkening to the mayor's entreaty.
Took Amtrak—in the carriage with "no talk."
My cab driver was turbaned and Pakistani.

At the Michelangelo, I had my normal suite
and met an old flame from my London days.
We dined well at Bouterin—an East Side retreat—
then tried to make love, but it wasn't the same.

Sunday, we went south to Canal and the Square
but it was blocked off by blue barricades.
Smudged photos of Dad and the colour of his hair,
a weird thought of ticker tape and parades.

That afternoon, a Broadway matinee
previewing Strindberg's *Dance of Death*.
Does one old life really matter today?
Will Sir Ian McKellen still draw breath?

The curtain came down to a long ovation,
but we hurried out before the next call.
An English discomfort at over-congratulation
and where the next axe might fall.

Then I remembered I had a dream
or was it a thought in the approaching train?
That I still saw the Twin Towers gleam
in the late sun, or was it early evening rain?

Down Fifty-Second for the ritual Ruby
and into a booth with a view of the fish.
I said, "The tikka and naan will do fine for me."
You had masala in a copper dish.

We sat in silence, sipping our beers,
and touched hands to prove we were still here.
The way dark-eyed peasants, weary with years,
resist the inevitable drawing near.

You kissed me goodbye and drove up your side.
I went the other way, down to the station.
To Philadelphia and another train ride,
struggling with the crossword in this week's *Nation*.

Putting it down, I looked out at the spruce and fir
and felt the unruliness of being alive.
The cut-out coffins where our hearts once were,
the possibilities of being able to arrive.

PATRICK

In the black June night,
the white speck of your tiny eyes.
Moonlight in the jungle.
I walk the room with you,
watching you for a sign;
a tired yawn,
a limp arm.
But in this black room,
your eyes follow mine
in a complexity of light.
Father and son,
we watch each other
tangled in our own lines,
the myriad of our cells.
I watch,
waiting for you to sleep
wishing the sequence
of our breathing
could become one.
I watch you grow
and wonder
at this strange
and disturbing energy.
You are my son
and I love you
but sometimes
I'm afraid.
I will rock you
till your hydrocephalic lids
consume each tiny moon
and we will be safe again.
Until tomorrow.

ODE TO ALAN AND
THE BLACK TAXI

I think you would agree
that there is poetry
everywhere you look …
e.g., take the *Blue Book*.

It's number sixteen of eight -
absolutely can't be late.
Eight o'clock St. Martins curtain;
knows his way round, that's for certain.

Out of Bricklayers, cut the talk,
then on the right, take Page's Walk.
By now you understand the code;
make a left on Tower Bridge Road.

Now Kent to the Elephant in his head,
on to St. Georges, the Good Book said.
But Al knows he needs to be thorough,
And his secret plan is Harper to Borough!

Whatever the chosen route, you can bet
Waterloo Bridge before the sun has set.
Over the river to Lancaster Place,
The Strand, Southampton Street, gathering pace.

Until Covent Garden is in his sight;
then Henrietta, Bedford on the right.
Bear left on Garrick to St. Martins Lane.
The "Upper" of course, that is plain.

On the left, West Street comes into view,
a bright theater hosting a revue.
"And here we are Guv' with time to spare."
I smiled and put a tenner on the fare!

ROBERT W GREEN

ONCE

I am old.
No tattoos
no piercings
Zero chains
around my neck
and my chest
hairless and bony
as a boy's.
Once
I had three of them
under the radar.
All sweet,
thin-limbed lads;
arms, knees, elbows
and then one suddenly gone.

COOKIES AND CANDIES

The familiarity
of Hope and See.
The new year
now well in.
A box
and biscuit tin.
One lonesome
mandarin,
his despondency
for all to see.
That quiet,
sad reflection,
a few, short weeks
of rejection.
The streamer's
shiny grin
ornates the orange
of his skin.
A single circle
fills the hole
magnified
in a crystal bowl.
It reminds me
how much
I count on you
to take this
safely
into twenty two.

TO LOUISE GLUCK

No,
you are not
the beauty of what
is not enough.
You are of no use
in the face
of the maple
turning.
Like all of us -
incompetent
to restore it.
But now,
in the hour
before another
rabid sunset,
your candor
or whatever
is of no mind
in the undeniable
humor
of Tanglewood
tonight, when
people laugh
in the luscious
sense of sound,
smell, and
postponed parties
of death
by association.

LOVE POEM

The silence
of worn stone
encompassing
footsteps
at a half open door.
Long shadows
seep into the reach
of an unadorned altar.
I sense your bare arm
brush against
the sleeve of my shirt.
Glancing
at your face,
I catch four
perfect diamonds—
blue, green,
brown and gold
follow one another
across the nape
of your neck.
I'm not sure
whether or not
that's a smile
but it goes
a long way back
to summers
in Clare
and the way
the hay
lingered longingly
in your hair.

ROBERT W GREEN

SWIM

when I
finally
get out
of the
water
head gone
exhausted
the sun
on my
stomach
catching
the bits
of water
my hands
reaching
for my
face
pushing
the skin
into my
hair
my hair
into my
back
my back
waiting
again
for the
feel of
the water

MOORE

What's the score
Judge Ray Moore?
Who's vulnerable
and poor?
What young girl
feels hurt and sore?
What takes you
outside the law?
Leave the Courthouse door
Judge Ray Moore -
Go back and run
some small Texas store;
You might win the battle
but never the war.

A SWEET

Late autumn sunshine.
Dead leaves
glittering on a lake.
A mauve dusk
heavy with vengeance.
One child
in each hand,
walking up a hill,
answering questions.
"The leaves drop off
because they're tired
of the same old tree."
"Better to be
of the same old tree
than drown in the lake."
At the top of the hill,
resting for a little while,
huddled together,
thinking of a diversion.
"The first one to touch
[they are already half way there]
the tree
gets a sweet."
"Not now,
when we get back
home."
The wind blows up.
The children laughing
at their hair
falling across their faces.
The leaves
forming into drifts
in the half darkness.
The sun disappearing
over the edge
of the water.

FATHER AND DAUGHTER

My brother bought me
the red and yellow CD
just for the first track.
I play it back to back
and foxtrot to it with you.
You love the bit that goes "Aahoogh."
Making Paul Simon's day,
cheek to cheek we sway
to the rhythm of the band.
Your tiny, chapped hand
clutches my finger so tight
as daylight makes way for night.
"Today is the solstice," I say.
You repeat the word in your head
and then stumbling over the S's,
you lisp to my caresses
of your soft, smiling face,
and putting me in my place,
chuckle with monster glee,
"Daddee sillee; Daddee sillee."

MEMORIAL SUNDAY, PHILADELPHIA, MAY 1996

Primroses shuddering
in the early evening
drizzle. Clouds
skidding across
the Delaware River.
On Penn's Landing,
the sounds of
the Jambalaya Jam
and the distant
recollection
of a Bo Diddley
number.
The semicircular
arrangement of
brick tears
and the sixties' riff
of a side percussion
add a sense
of sadness,
of desertion.
The marble
gives way
to names
embedded
in strict
alphabetical order.
From "Adams
John W."
to "Zybrinski
Alan K."
And facing them,
tableaus
of places
that are not
American.
Hua Dong and
Qua Tini,
where D Division
was ambushed.
The soft shower
becomes rain,
and the beat
becomes
more insistent.
"Hand jive,
do that crazy
hand jive …"
The traffic roars
down 95,
and I am still
alive. We walk
away. Hand in hand.
Toward another
promised land.

SOPHIE

sophie
you live
and breathe
in a world
and space
that I
cannot
influence
or control
and I'm
sorry if
this sounds
like
surrender.
and don't
get me
wrong,
I am
seriously
pissed
about it
but one day
down some
fabled
yellow brick
road,
all that
may change.
But today
all I can
realistically
do is to
hold you
firmly in
my arms
and let
your lovely
bony brain
rest against
my chest
and hear

the ticktock
of your
beating
heart
employ
the skin
of my belly,
like a
celtic
bodhrain
and make
you smile
when day
light cracks
rectangles
through our
white slats,
and I let
you sit on
top of me
and pull
my hair
and tweak my
ungrabbable
nipples.
And then
the chuckle
of your deep
and dirty
monster
laugh as
you spy
my watch
crumpled
silver on
the stand
and say,
"dadadah,"
before you go
dive bombing
over the edge

ROBERT W GREEN

of the bed,
and I have
to catch
your ankle
before
we detonate
our bombs
on some more
helpless
afghan
babies on
their way
to border
camps too
tired and
hungry
to cry
in their
mothers
skinny arms
whose one
wish is
to miss
the land
mines and
cluster
bombs
that litter
each dirt
road
and I pull
you back
from the
brink
and kiss
your head
because
that is what
it still is,
and I think
of corridors,

not of infant
or preschool
classes, but
of baghdad
lanes, where
B47s patrol
and punish
iraqi
children
for having
the nerve
to still have
someone
called
saddam
as their
father
or of strike
zones
around
kabul and
kandahar,
where there
are no
targets left,
so we
destroy
mud houses
hospitals,
and red cross
depots
only because
we can, and
now your
startled yell
tells me I'm
clutching you
too tightly,
and tears
are streaming
down my face.

PARTING

Chris,
is this amiss?
No goodbyes.
My eyes
ache so.
No,
don't say
it's all okay.
Will you bring
everything?
A book, a key,
a bit of me?
Remember the flat,
my Irish hat?
Your funny toes,
a worn out rose?
Will you kiss me?
Even miss me?
There's no one to tell.
Farewell,
fly away
to another day.
All sunshine and blue.
The new one I promised you.

RETURN

I need
to get back
to the sea.
On a stone
doorstep
that opens up
to the Atlantic
that would lead me
down the bohreen
to the wild blackberries
and the tears of God.
There is no anarchy
in this ocean.
Only a relentless,
invasion
of flat repetition.
A conspiracy of
smiling skies
and sheep filled meadows
that makes me reconsider.
Reconsider.

FOR ROSS

In ninety-nine when you are twenty one
I wish you the rain, the wind, and the sun
or will it be moons, holographs, and laser phones;
pulstars, plasmids, and genetic cones?

Perhaps it will be Cambridge, London, or Trinity,
fronting a rock band or reading divinity.
Or will it be the pub in Main Street, Killarney
with pints of Guinness and the old man's blarney?

May you have crocuses, snowdrops, and the smell of spring;
may you wake to hear robins and chaffinches sing.
May you wonder at the Slieve Mish and walk on the strand,
swim in the sea, and ride horses on the sand.

Only one thing to remember when you read this—
you started life as a rather long kiss
back in seventy-seven in the month of May -
it's ninety-nine and love still rules—OK?

ROBERT W GREEN

FOR SARAH

Was it really as long ago as that
in your navy blue uniform and matching hat
that we walked to St. Gilda's at ten to nine
your trusting fingers entwined in mine?

But proud and sure even then
at seven, eight, nine, and ten.
The years scurried past like April skies,
blurred greys and mauves and crimplene ties.

A thought before that of when you were three
and the youngest kid in the nursery
with that snuggling hat and saucy eyes
the frost, the pushchair, and Hornsey Rise.

And primary schools remembered still
and Channing High on Highgate Hill
with buses now replaced by cars
smiles in the back, checking your stars.

And so to Kerry where our hearts took hold;
the Milltown nuns thought you were far "too bold".
Laughing with Norma till your sides would ache
about the domestic class and the well-done steak!

On next to Joe and Killorglin town
the dusty old bus from Ballinagroun
the trek with Dan up the long bohreen
and now you're well past seventeen.

With final exams and late-night revision
with future hopes and days of decision
but sometimes I wish it could be like then
and we would hold hands tightly - once again…

May 1980

HI, NICK

What a world
we have for you!
Your soldierly flax,
your eyes of blue.
Hi, Nick!
Welcome here
to Ballinagroun.
Your gentle smile,
your cautious frown.
Hi, Nick!
It's Grandpop here—
the crackly voice,
the smell of beer.
Hey, Nick,
look at that photo
on the wall,
when you were just
two feet tall.
That's me and you
in a pose
for posterity,
I suppose.
So long, Nick.
Sorry I had to run
before the fun
had really begun.

ROBERT W GREEN

TOES

The skin
peels back
like a papery
flake of filo.
See me.

See now
how poor I am.
See now
how unnecessary
it all was…

You should have
taken note of my toes.
Oh,
the aristocracy
of separate toes!

Take off
the handmade shoes
and lo—
the way they
stick together…

And now
a surprise prize
for white
ivory fingers
unzip the gloves

Maestro,
let us see
your crinkled tendons
your deaf
stump.

GALLERY

Exuberant
pink petals
float in pure glass
down to the spindly roots
of tiny earth figures
splayed out,
naked
and vulnerable.
I remember
your expression
peering through
a magnifying glass,
concentrating
on the finely spun wing
of an immaculate bee.
Alone
with thoughts of you
and the foreboding
presence
of the work of strangers,
I wander aimlessly
down to the sombre
charcoals.
In a series
of smears
in a quiet corner
at the back,
a bird with a beak
becomes a man,
a crucifix.

ROBERT W GREEN

FRANCES

Dear Frances,
the odds
are chances.
Physically
and aerodynamically
it is totally
impossible
for a bee to fly.
The weight
of the body
and the flimsy
wings, you see.

Of course,
the suspensory
ligaments
of the horse
means it cannot
bear the tons
it has to carry
when it runs.

Love, therefore,
will not occur.
But in case
it does,
just buzz
like a bee
in some flowery place;
and blur
your soul
like the flash
of colour
at the three-
furlong pole!

IRIDESCENT STAR

At what point
does the back
bit of our brain
interrupt
the ducts behind
the white globs
of our eyelids?
My eldest son
is dead.
Knocked out
by blows
to the head.
Brown bread,
donated organs
and how
do you fathom
it's still him?
Oh no more.

Show me
the door
to the back
of the church.
What is left?
Britta, Nick,
not bereft
but looking
from the strand
to the sea.
That holding
of shoulders.
You and me.
Walk me home
to where
you are—
that bright,
iridescent star.

FREEDOM

The scar
is as scary
as the thought
of a new
freedom.
The abdomen
still sore,
fragile
to her fingers
but now
the realization
that she had it
all along.
A breaking bad
desert
open to all
the elements;
cultivate
a cactus;
be a scorpion.
And she gets it.
The sand sailing
she took

for granted.
No kids
to pick up;
parents
long gone
and the weary
dispersal
of old friends.
Smiling
to herself,
she recites
rhymes from
her kindergarten.
Humpty Dumpty;
Hickory, Dickery, Dock.
Through the ward
window sills,
beyond
a parking lot,
scrubby trees
give way
to boundless
Sierra hills.

MUSINGS FROM LA CALACA FELIZ, 11/8/21

Where in my head
are the words
I'd forgotten.
The unfinished
poems
on the back
of paper napkins,
buried
in the third drawer.
It is the first day
since the clocks
were turned back.
A reverse stirring
of events;
a chill,
November darkness
before the day's
first g and t.
You and me,
separated by years;
joined up
by dried up tears
of two young mothers,
dead before
their time.
Where does
the soft pileup
of unswept leaves
belong
in all of this?
Memories
of summer
or perhaps within
the last
goodbye kiss.

JUNE

an evening in june
it rains incessantly
i am wasting my time
the fact
that the sky is deep blue
luminous
the dumb
quick
contact
of the rain
on the stone steps
and the rooftops
it is hopeless
the soft shoots of new grass
i want to break in
how still
the trees
everything
is complete
held in this loose
unbreakable skin
like an oxygen
tent I get
the feeling
he never
makes mistakes

JOURNEY

1

framed in a classic
arched bridge
over number one
california state highway
the rain in your face
the pacific powering in
at your back and
the river running fast
through the tall pines
to capture the corner
of the lens -
click
and the imprint
of your smile
already locked
in my negative

2

Into grey darkening
skies and the hollow
sounds
of distant surf,
we rode the
Russian river
into Jenner.
The cowboy sweep
of the water,
the carefree curve
of the road
merging into

the implacable
ledge of the sea.
You remain quiet,
watchful,
anticipating
the night ahead.

3

not because
of how beautiful
you are
looking across
a table
in Mendocino
through an old
perrier bottle
of lilac and lemon
wildflowers,
but one day,
when the fly wires
of our world
are free
we will become
our own
point conception
a sunlit
shadowless
totem pole
of life
and something else

4

Riding
the redwoods
from Fort Bragg

to Willets,
weaving valley
and forest,
another
journey.
Treetop shafts
of blue and
grey light
the crackle
quietness
of the
conifers.
Willie Nelson
on FM.
The way
you smile
behind the
wheel.

5a

I am
at Noyo,
saying your name
in your wet hat,
making plans
for part b.
Driving home
through the
rainswept road,
snug secure
in our ocean mist.
And then,
this is it.

ROBERT W GREEN

5b

Back at town hall
in Heritage House,
playing Scrabble
in front of
a log fire;
cookies, red wine,
and words
as the waves
close in.

5c

In bed
a short time later,
you turn on
your elbow,
tell me
about your world,
and the way I am.
Chastened,
I begin
a fitful sleep
on the
far reaches
of the pillow.

6

Arguing
through blinds
in the latticework,
the pale sun
moves round
the Scandia

and settles quietly
on the fig trees.
Unconvinced,
you leave
the table
with a start
and renew
your blood-brown lipstick.

7

This is the end
of a journey.
Driving back
from the Getty
through Malibu,
your hand
on my knee,
the placid
sun-dappled sea
singing
your sweet praises,
hiding for now
the leagues and fathoms
of the valley below.

ROBERT W GREEN

NORMA JEAN

My period was heavy, and I went to the cemetery early
in the morning. The birds were singing, and two men were
working on the far side, furthest from the road. It was
near where they had buried Ana on a sunless afternoon
last Friday. This day was a bit brighter but cold,
with a breeze ruffling the cut flowers on the freshly
filled graves. The men were digging a new plot for
the morning's business. They had reached a depth where
they needed a ladder to climb up and down. I
walked over to them and looked into the hole.
I asked if I could get down there. "Sure," they said,
smiling. Then they looked at each other, and they looked
at me in the way men have done for the last two years now.
I hitched my skirt and climbed in.

At the bottom, I lay down and looked up. The earth
was still damp, and I could feel the numb coldness
through the sweater on my back. My nipples were stiff,
and the sky was one secure oblong. There was so much in
that piece of blue-grey sky that it was quite a view. I
lay there, thinking of Ana and myself and what it must be
like to be down here as cold and alone as this. I know I would
be fifteen in two weeks' time, but I didn't know anything. Not
properly anyhow. I stood up and climbed out. The men
wanted to fool around, but I walked away,
back toward the other place.
I said to myself, "Something will happen. I just know it."

WHERE DO YOU GO?

Tonight I am
that bird
looking for
a dark place
to die.
A dense bush
at the end
of the wood;
or the low,
thick branches
of an ancient oak
would be nice.
In the air,
seamless
over deep-hanging
clouds,
the freedom
of unlimited
flight—
the way
I lived
my life,
flashing
my cardinal red
from the edge
of a cliff
in Truro
to some skyscraper
in Manhattan.
It doesn't matter
but good
to know
when it's time
to go.
The neurosis
of the land,
pick-pecking
our path for
shaded bread crumbs.
And then
the watchful eye
of a hairless
cat, waiting
that moment
to pounce.
Let me fly
one more time
into that envelope
of air above
the brim
of the ocean
and then disappear
forever
into the darkest
green of lichen
I can find.

JUVENILIA (PRE 1960)

TONIGHT

Tonight
an old man
on a bicycle
pedals toward me.
He is leant forward,
following the
flat, misshapen
circle of light
advancing along the road.

Gold-ringed
flabby-fingered men
in their new two-tone Consuls,
smelling of money
and looking sour.

NORTH CIRCULAR

In this space,
in this time even,
unrelated I
burn the air.
Time climbs
unscalable walls,
The yellow grass withers
on the building site.
The wind rises
out of the dust craters.
The desolate hoardings
fly backwards by
a million cars.
The news of the
old people's
community center
as it gets dark.
Unable to move,
I stand at the edge
of the foundation pits
and watch their headlights
scan the north circular.

SURVIVORS

There was a way
we walked toward each other.
A sense
of distance,
unmeasured
but still a number
of steps. Do
you see a sign?
A long line
coming over a hill?
A wall
we cannot see the start of?
Do not be afraid.
It was made
by us long ago.
A flat stone.
Once
it was round.

THE CIRCLE

The space limps between my lines.
A circle, a square,
a mad arrow.
Will you still love me in the morning?
Will you smile?

My circle has improved.
A single line, drawn quickly.
Tonight I broke it
with a thin line.
It became alive, lonely.
I love you.
Do you know that?

I saw a cat tonight,
walking unusually slowly
along the street.
Head up, eyes bright.
I think of you.
Will the world wait for us?

LANDSY

I know what it's like for him,
but what can you say?
Sitting over a beer with him today,
I thought, *It's pointless telling him*
not to worry. There's nothing
really except to hope that it's OK.
And if it's not, well, just pray
that he doesn't do something
stupid. I ask if he wants another beer.
He shakes his head; "Let's get out of here,"
he says, and so we go down
by the river and watch the gulls drifting around.
I say to him, "It'll probably be all right, mate."
"All right," he says, "when she's already two weeks late?"

ASTROWORLD

The sounds crowd in,
narrowing the margin.
One upon one
they come,
reaching a peak.
Don't speak.
Stalked by disaster,
I understand this:
Something sinister
awaits us.

ROBERT W GREEN

ELEANOR

Snap!
Your back
snaps.
The spine
of the glass
dangles
from my fingers
a fragment
of pain.

Crack!
The morning
cracks.
The curtains
close in,
give us
massive
blocks
of darkness
to play in.

THE ADVANCE

I walk down the street.
No contact.
Surrounded by air,
I stand
at the edge of a desert,
still.
Perhaps a sound.
The presence of these houses,
dark.
The wind,
slight,
rising out of the line
of the sky
every time I move.
The sound
of children playing,
cars reversing,
people I know
talking to me
suspended.
The way the eye
tries to take in
the desert,
spring the edge,
the terrible advance.
I walk down the street
and watch
the evil buds
rear their deadly heads
for the last time.

ROBERT W GREEN

THE DRUMMER

The drummer sits erect
in a white suit.
His brushes clip a cymbal.
The pianist,
his head on one side,
leans back,
winces at the pause
of his own chords,
then strikes again
like a chameleon.
We touch hands
in the darkness.
Our isolated notes
thread through
the smoke
in a strange
progression.

SPRING

Once I was alive.
I awoke in the morning
early, and yes,
I was alive.
Any digit would react,
record,
press any button.
Yes,
I would work.
My skin
molecular.
The spring grass
devoured by dew.
I can't help it.
That is what it was like.
But how sour
the sound of
cutting flutes?
No sense
in putting things
straight.
Anyway,
I am unable.
Goodbye.
What does it matter?
Once
we were alive.
It was too painful,
but it doesn't matter.
It doesn't matter.

ROBERT W GREEN

THIS MORNING

Spring slows down
into summer.
The days hang around
too long,
like blossom on the pavements.

I awake
at four in the morning.
The birds screech.
It is already light.
It could be yesterday again.

I cannot tell you
how much my brain aches.
I am alive,
and I am trapped
by the living.

THE ANSWER

Lying there
Half asleep,
You are the evening lake
At Veernigen.
Undisturbed,
Motionless.
I am the man who steals up.
Holds his breath,
Ripples his finger
Through the soft warm water
And waits for an answer
To appear in your eyes.

ROBERT W GREEN

MIRAMARE

Miramare awoke
and opened like a flower.
Slowly,
like the shutters
slipping into their folds
step by step by step
across each track
where dust already gathered.

BEACH

"How many times must I tell you?"
Alone,
One child's face
In the unconcerned
Holiday crowd.
The pier,
The sand,
The cell of a tear
Beginning to form.

KIDS

Along the street
Small children play at war,
Shrieking their machine-gun fire
And hiding behind walls.

One of them staggers,
Falls gloriously to the pavement,
Clutching his heart.

THE FLY

It is early summer;
Or perhaps it is nearly midsummer.
A length of curtain
That covers the scullery
Rustles the stone floor.
(It is cool in there.)

A restless fly lives
Only because I cannot be bothered
To get up and kill it.
It takes a chance and circles my arm.
My fingers do nothing
Except grasp the empty air.

ROBERT W GREEN

ANDY

My brother's a clever bloke for six.
At school they teach him tricks,
like doing his shoelaces up and telling the time.

They say
my uncle Block is round the twist.
He's got one glass eye
and smokes a clay pipe.

HYPNOSIS

I dribble
my sputum
into
a little
tin mug,
and
the doctor
is looking
at me
with
tired,
grey
eyes.
The girl
from the path lab
comes in
and
I think,
What
a nice
seamless
leg

she has.
She goes.
The cavity
is perfectly clear.
"In your case,
I think
it's nerves,"
he says.
There are footsteps
across the wing.
I look
at the door,
but
they carry
straight on.
"She's married,"
he says.
"Come back
a week
today.
We'll try
hypnosis."

LONDON

Small houses
tending to darkness.
A solitary light
burning at the corner.
Their assimilation.

An outline of railway trees,
the sound of rain on tarpaulin.

THAT'S HOW IT'S GONNA BE

Who am I
sitting here,
lulled to a past emotion
by the incessant banality
of a three-year-old
Buddy Holly record,
remembering
the darkness
of the Hollywood Club
and liking the cold feeling
in my belly
and the way the collar
of my black suede jacket stood up
and the line of my legs
in tight grey jeans,
and thinking
maybe tonight,
maybe?

ROBERT W GREEN

OCTOBER

As it begins to get dark,
Several unobtrusive mists
Slip through the town trees
And haze the lights at the end of the street.
At first,
October is a deceptive month.

MODERN JAZZ

The line of her long white neck
Startles the fold of blue velvet.
Dangerously soft.
The snake pearl dress ring
And the glass shudders.
Martini on the rocks,
And Miles Davis plays silver.

THE BANK

Every afternoon
at half past two,
thirteen stories
of tight grey brick
begin to press my brain
into the pit of my balls.

1960

It was the first Sunday in February,
And the sun shone for the first time this year.
It was as though it had never shone before.
It came ice cold in an early morning
Ice-blue sky,
And the shadows were sharp and pointed.
They call this year 1960,
And perhaps I can look forward.

ROBERT W GREEN

THE STAIRS

She stood upon the stairs
As though she would take another step down.
Her arms poised forward,
And her knee slipping away to the darkness
Of the step before.
But all that moved
Were the shadows across the slope of her stomach
And the slight tremble of her shoulder.
I remember
How I tried to move her
And how I could feel her wanting
To pass through
To the step below.
But that first night
She and everything seemed like a religion.
And for days after,
I would see her,
Transparent
On every stair.

LOCUSTS

Walking home tonight she saw a tree
with clusters of April buds upon it.
"Look," she said, "do you see
the orange butterflies?
Every one of them has wings and a little brown head."
"They are locusts," I said.

NETS

The flicker of your eye
against my lips.

Small fish swim
and are caught by fishermen.

Out of the still, blue sea
they rise from the nets.

Their silver breasts twist and sully,
making tiny scratches on the sky.

The sun goes down,
casting long and beautiful shadows.

The nets lay drying
on the golden sands.

These then
are the happy
blistered hands.

SOME THOUGHTS AT CHRISTMAS

A big armchair
Sitting there.
"Not so much tonic this time, Tom."
"A gin and lime, dear?"
There is a clink of glasses far away.
The pattern on the lampshade may

be shadows made by decorations.
Her arm around my neck.
Falling forward.
Limp and white.
Christmas night.
Calm and bright.

As though Christmas lay in a valley,
I could see the lights from the top of the hill.
And I ran to them as a child,
Hopeful and with open eyes.
And all the time really knowing.

ROBERT W GREEN

SPRINGTIME

The soft rain of a late April evening
Slowly uncovers a hidden universe
That I had never seen before.
Without manner or purpose,
It seems to reflect
The frightening wonder
Of ordinary things.

ITALY

I turned
And saw her standing there.
Her face against the sky.
A slender quarter moon
Slipped through the evening clouds.
And the sea met the night in gentleness
To the music of Boccherini
Playing below.

ROBERT W GREEN

THE WALL

When they come
and the bolts are loosed
and the fly wires
of the brain
are free,
when the birds fly
and the rabbits are released,
when the cabbages grow
and the grass is green,
when the pavements smell sweet again
after rain, and the concrete pools of light
contain the sound
of people sleeping,
when the beers run out
and monks on blue note
building blue-colored bricks,
when they burn my dark glasses,
and I build my wall to China
and find some more beer,
and they break my wall
and I am a spider
hiding from the birds
within the bricks
that we broke,
I wish they hadn't have come,
and the rabbits
were still
in wire cages.

TWO POEMS FOR KIDS

THE RAT AND THE CAT

A rat
came to town.
He wore a gown
and flat hat.
He set up a school.
A cat came to look,
took a book,
and felt like a fool.
The rat who
was fat
told the cat
it was cool
to come to school
and learn what's what.
The cat said,
"I sit so still;
I hunt and kill.
I eat and sleep,
but I'm no creep!"
The rat wore a smile
as long as a mile.
"You need to read,
do math, and spell,
learn to write
and count as well."
"How much,"
said the cat,
"to do all that?"
"I'm not mean.
I won't charge you
a bean,"
said the rat.
"But you must come
each day,
turn your back
on play,
and hear what I say."
"OK,"
said the cat.

"It's a deal.
I'll do my best
and put in the time.
I'll wear the class vest
and learn how to rhyme.
But do not
lose sight
of one fact
in this phase
that cats,
like it or not,
get set in their ways."
Days
went to weeks
and then to a year.
The rat taught
all he knew
from his tail
to his ear.
And the cat
learned things
he had not known.
He could read
and write
and talk on the phone!
One day
the rat said,
"The role
of the soul
is to seek
what's right.
To find light
in the night
and to make
what is black,
white."

"Will I get it
or what?"
said the cat.
"I think not,"
said the rat,
and in a flash,
he knew
his days were gone
up high in the sky.
That he would be
the mash
for the cat's next pie.
And as you all
know by now,
the cat ate the rat
and how!

The last word,
of course,
comes from the cat:
"I learned all
I had to know,
and that was that.
I think
life
is a set of doors;
you go through them,
wink,
and lick
your paws!"

ROBERT W GREEN

THE FIGHT

This is a long-lasting contest
between the land and the sea.
Celebrity herons ringside,
the sky a tuxedoed referee.

The scrubby, chiseled challenger
with bone rock-fingered fists,
the cunning, conniving champion
with wild, wet, wavy wrists.

The moon is in sea's corner,
whip whipping up the surf.
The earth is scheming strategy
while sandbagging sacks of turf.

Fights have contradictions
of loons and cricket cries.
Players are not what they seem
and could be secret spies.

A twisted river, lake, and stream
hide inside earth's training ground.
A reef and archipelago
can penetrate the deepest sound.

"Seconds out, round 1," the sky intones
as they edge to the center of the ring.
Feeling each other out with ripple and stone
in their ambition to become the King.

The opening curtain is Ireland
and its fierce West Kerry shore.
The land still tilled by grizzled hands,
the black sod drying in the store.

The sea builds up some hungry waves,
laced with spit-stinging spray.
Dingle braces for the worst,
its headland hard into the bay.

The sea has thrown its sucker punch,
but the earth is no one's fool.
The sunlight swaddles houses,
and Blasket winks at Coumeenoole.

Back in the deep blue corner,
the cut man gets called in.
Neptune, the champ's manager says,
"That was Slea Head's jagged chin."

Patched up and pounding to go,
the ocean roars into round 2.
Land climbs wearily from its stool,
ruminating on what to do.

South of Miami, Florida,
the scenery is the Keys.
Urged on by a tropical,
the fathoms smash the trees.

Palm fronds litter the howling street.
The deserted bars are shut.
The sea surges for a knockout.
The earth is one big rut.

Then the surly storm subsides,
leaving just a muddy mound.
Key West regains its foothold
but clearly, the champion's round.

The inter-round mannequin
parades around the ring;
her ample chest heaves out
as she spies promoter King.

Sitting front row center,
his hair two stories high,
writing numbers in a notebook,
and grinning at the sky.

Round 3 begins slowly
as the combatants regain their breath.
They know this will be a long one—
maybe till the death.

The backdrop is Australia,
that forgotten land down under,
where hope burns with a passion,
and dreams are torn asunder.

The sea starts off quite bravely
with a Tasman Timor one two.
Then it pincers for the kidney
with Pacific Indian blue.

Seven surf sneaks into frame
attacking Wollongong.
The green highlands stand upright
and sing a victory song.

Now the earth is bloody red
from a noon-high scorching sun.
It shows its stringy muscles
as it knows the round is won.

The sand and stone and crystal
don't dwell upon such things.
You have to be as hard as nails
when your name is Alice Springs.

The cut man's back upon the scene.
The grey trainer rants and raves.
"You need this round real bad, m'boy,
try some stomach-crunching waves."

The ring this time heads northbound
to the frozen Arctic lands,
where there is no day or night,
the sea gloves its cunning hands.

Instead of waves it brings warmth,
a slight, insidious heat.
The permafrost loses ground
and knows when it is beat.

The score cards now look even
after a boring, slow round 4.
The land is thinking, *Let's attack.*
The sea wonders what's in store.

The white ropes reveal round 5
and its unlikely destination.
The sea needs the rivers' help
when it feels earth's determination.

The backdrop is the Netherlands
and project reclamation.
The Rhine, Scheldt, and Meuse
rise up in exclamation!

A cold North Sea meets the delta
as the tides try to do their worst.
Straining to recover territory,
hoping that the dams will burst.

But the dogged dykes hold firm
powered by pumps in numbers,
using its opponent's steam
to grow tulips and cucumbers.

So the polders stay drained,
showing the land can box clever too.
Turning the sea's strength back on itself
was a pretty smart thing to do.

A third of the way through the fight,
with another ten rounds to go,
they both dig down into the depths
of their hidden reserves below.

Miss Heaving Mammary herself
glides around the canvas mess,
parading the card for round 6.
It says, simply, the US.

From Philly to Columbus,
Detroit and Kansas City,
Denver, Vegas, and LA,
Where, "You know who," are pretty.

Overheard at ringside,
among the knowing crowd,
a reporter to a showgirl
whispers rather loud,

"That's a bit of a stretch,
taking on his solar plexus.
What's the game plan here?
An Atlantic/Pacific nexus?"

"Wrong ring location," calls the ref,
who is, by the way, terrific.
"Venues were agreed in advance;
they have to be site-specific."

A hasty conference takes place
between the rival camps.
The California coast
is agreed to between the ramps.

So we head out to Big Sur,
to Carmel and Monterey.
The sea is roaring, "Get back."
The cypress groans, "No way."

This is Clint Eastwood country,
smoking cheroots and acting mean.
But looking tough is not enough
when the sea starts turning green.

It pounds into the skinny rocks
and crunches the darkening sand.
It attacks the coastal grasses
like a driving, punkish band.

ROBERT W GREEN

It's nasty, black, and violent
as the referee shakes his head.
Upon the battered headland
the withered tree is dead.

The round goes to the champion,
and that is no surprise.
The lazy land dropped its guard
and got smacked between the eyes.

The cornerguys are busy
with bucket, sponge, and grease.
The fighters slumped upon their stools
wish hostilities would cease.

But it's now the seventh round,
and neither one can flounder.
Every ounce of stamina
goes into a fifteen-rounder.

The scenery change for seven
is really quite dramatic.
We swap the windswept pines
for the Balkan Adriatic.

Where race and religion smolder,
rivers and vengeance run rife.
Bosnia, Kosovo, Serbia—
the land is torn by strife.

This looks easy for the sea
as the earth breaks out in a fit.
Guns from Zagreb to Dubrovnik,
death in Sarajevo and Split.

The sea sweeps down the coastline
through the peninsula chain.
Raising its level silently,
increasing the opponent's pain.

But this land has been around
for many centuries past.
Bloodstains baked into the ground
and stones and spires that last.

The UN is on patrol,
peacekeeping the borderlines,
allowing villagers to survive
by defusing enemy mines.

And pain has toughened its sinews,
so the earth can stare down defeat.
It embraces wrinkled peasants
and the homeless in bare feet.

The sea comprehends this spirit,
and as a tactical fighter,
backpedals the rest of the round,
thinking, *Introduce something lighter.*

The fast quip, well-read crowd
are savvy but with feeling.
They know the works of Hazlitt,
Egan, and A. J. Leibling.

And Mailer, too, come to that,
wrote of an epic Zaire fight.
In the night air of Kinshasa
when Ali took on Foreman's might.

And that long list of pugilists
stretching back to Regent times,
but nothing like these warriors
globe knuckling through various climes.

So we sashay into the eighth,
the sea looking dreamy with sleep.
A lapping of a distant shore;
what a blissful sense of the deep.

The setting is Bangladesh,
on the coast by Chittagong.
Its water buffalo tethered,
the lone herdsman hums a song.

The sun slips through the mangroves;
a coconut sways on its palm.
The earth stretches and relaxes,
but the air is ominously calm.

It is a late September evening,
and the earth knows not what to do.
The Bay of Bengal is glassy
till it hears plops of rain on bamboo.

In minutes the heavens have parted;
a torrent is unleashed on the plain.
The elephants snort in pleasure
at the relentless, restless rain.

The Karnaphuli is bubbling;
the river's bank will break.
Benny scowls a wicked grin
and says, "Brother, let's make a lake."

The rocks of shale are soft;
the soil is saline clay.
The earth relies on Kaptai dam
and prays that it won't give way.

The waters come together
in a great big moving tide,
flash flooding the fertile coastland,
taking the Sundarbans for a ride.

And so the round is over;
the land looks for some release.
It's submerged into submission,
the contest tied at four a piece.

The cornermen are whispering
into cauliflower ears.
Pleading, wheedling, and needling,
minders on the verge of tears.

But rising for the ninth,
their "boys" look refreshed and trim.
Assigned to fight on new terrain,
they hide each aching limb.

The illustrious crowd ringside
includes the signor Verdi,
a famous bookmaker poet,
rambunctious, sharp, and wordy.

He's made a special journey
for this championship bout
from his native Sicily,
his odds-making skills not in doubt.

ROBERT W GREEN

"Six to five on and evens.
a tie pays twenty to one."
The punters pile on with fistfuls,
backing their chosen one.

The wise guy from Palermo
knows where the value lies.
Balance your book on the two,
and a draw takes home the prize.

An 8 1/2 percent
theoretical "in the bin,"
really means a 100 percent
if neither one can win.

Now cherry blossoms fill the hall,
the mood is quite serene.
The setting is simply scenic,
the air Mount Fuji clean.

Japan's most northerly island,
Hokkaido is the place.
A land of magical mystery,
of cragginess and grace.

Of paddy fields and mountains,
green crops of delicate tea,
forests of sakhalin spruce,
the Ishikari running free.

But this air of tranquility
is deceptive to say the least.
The land can be quite murderous,
an untamed savage beast.

With earthquakes and volcano
lurking beneath its rim,
tidings for the Sea of Okhotsk
look decidedly grim.

It may have cyclonic storms
and fanatical typhoons,
but against earth's burning fissures,
its waves are punctured balloons.

And so the sea retreats,
suggesting an awkward peace,
but not without leaving
a squadron of spying geese.

As beaks are settled into down—
a quiet collective bed—
the sea smooths out without a frown;
true champions think ahead.

The sky looks at its scorecard,
old charts from academia,
like lost Sumerian scripts
from southern Mesopotamia.

(From the tenth round onward,
as any good pro will tell,
a boxer must impress
in the minute before the bell.)

So again they're squaring off,
sea lichen and ancient moss.
There's consequential jabbing
with the occasional right cross.

And they're center stage once more,
contained by pride and rope,
scrapping now in Africa
down at the Cape of Good Hope.

It starts deep in the ocean's heart,
a wave on a windswept ride,
and gathers fierce intensity—
a loathing of apartheid.

Whether Black, White, or Colored
means nothing to the sea.
Aegean, North, Red, or Dead,
we're all one family.

For the land here is divided,
which will not help its defense.
The bottom of South Africa
resembles a chain link fence.

Rottweiler dogs and truncheons
are out in the streets in force.
The sea tells Table Mountain,
"History will run its course."

And as the round wears on,
the existing order crumbles.
From their exalted perch
deceit and bigotry tumbles.

And the sea maintains its pressure,
pounding upon the shore,
reminding its opponent of who
really keeps the score.

This is one beautiful country,
and its people deserve a rest.
And though the land has lost the round,
it certainly was for the best.

From Cape Town to Johannesburg,
the folks play a singular note.
English, Fakir, or Afrikaans,
Soweto has an equal vote.

Round 11 is shaping up,
and rather than political,
the audience expectation
is for something far more physical.

And thus we find our foes
in a wild and rugged region.
This is as tough as it can get—
the topography Norwegian.

A few million years ago,
in the Ice Age glaciation,
rivers kicked off this round
that led to land's emaciation.

Roaring westward from gnarly peaks,
they sought out weakness in the ground,
carving gorges and steep fjords,
hooking their way coastward bound.

From Stavanger, Bergen, and Trondheim,
up to the Honningsvag flo,
the earth's face has been fractured
by scissoring punches, to and fro.

The land is badly slashed
by granite ravines and lakes.
A score of islands round its nose
a piteous beauty makes.

Yet the land has hardy people,
the Nordic and the Lapp.
They're Norway's hidden assets;
you can't see them on the map.

And though the sea has this round won,
there's ironic compensation.
For this land of fearless seamen
becomes a major shipping nation!

Thus they shuffle into the twelfth,
the last stages of the bout.
There's standing room only,
and one very happy ticket tout.

For a match like this is pricey,
and the fighters command huge fees.
The money's made outside the ring
on multitude pay TVs.

But players like their action live,
and the scalpers know this too.
Snaring blocks of good seat tickets,
a grand gets you a ringside view.

And their eyes are now glued
as the battle heads east once more,
to the lands of Southeast Asia
and a bustling Singapore.

But before a punch gets thrown,
up jumps a rep from PRC.
"My government protests.
You're not where you are meant to be.

The Global Fighting Union
mandate number 83,
says the venue of this round
must be Chinese terri-tory.

Singapore's population
is nearly all Chinese,
but not part of country
understand, if you please."

The night sky is embarrassed
and turns a crimson red.
Looks at the judge of rules
and asks, "Better red than dead?"

The ring official ponders
this difficult legal claim.
"1 think the consul makes his point.
The venue he can name."

The PRC ambassador
grins like the proverbial cat.
"I think you will appreciate
that Hong Kong is where it's at!"

A British ex-subaltern,
who always feared the worst,
is so apoplectic
his veins seem ready to burst.

Thoughts of his colonial past,
days of cricket on the green,
the slap of willow on leather,
and the way things might have been.

He mutters to those in earshot,
"Now we'll never get any peace.
We had to leave in ninety-seven
at the conclusion of our lease.

Then the centralists took over,
and therein lies the rub.
Men in light-grey tunics
had tables at the Jockey Club!"

But life moves on regardless;
anyone will tell you that.
So down to Victoria Harbour
to discover what pleased the cat.

And as round 12 progresses,
it soon becomes patently clear.
The land gets this one's measure
and has virtually nothing to fear.

It slams upward and outward,
in every single direction.
Skyscrapers jostle for space
built on the opium connection.

The waters retreat quickly
into the South China Sea.
Kwan Tong is now on land;
trade rules in Tsim Sha Tsui.

Indeed, commerce reigns supreme
throughout this Canton domain.
Aitch kay's four hundred square miles
has money, the port, and a brain.

So China is justly proud
of its contribution to the land.
And into this new century,
it raises its head from the sand.

For its prepenultimate spree
the earth concocts "plan audacious."
"Unlucky for some," says the sea.
Resistance will be tenacious."

The land has a master stroke
that, if coming to fruition,
would have the profoundest change
on McNally's latest edition.

"What if we were to join
our two most dominant places
and create this great behemoth
of five hundred million faces?"

Scramblers have been employed,
earth's secret to protect
from underwater devices
that are trying to detect.

The sea's bedded agents
break the sinister code
and put the Bering Strait
on colour red, defense mode.

That comparatively thin sliver
of icy cold water,
Russian signals to Alaska,
a mother to her daughter.

Now the leading question is
how do they bridge the divide?
By span and supporting ramparts
or culturally inside?

Or what about work and business
for prospectors and gold diggers?
Should Russians and Americans
be known as trappers and oil riggers?

The simple answer was given
some four decades afar.
When the Beatles did a Beach Boys
with "Back in the USSR."

Rock music was the common ground
built on a beat foundation.
For just three minutes at a time,
it joined nation unto nation.

The sea recognizes danger
and starts a whispering campaign.
Wavelengths dribble drops of fear
between each near-flung domain.

And before too long it's back—
the clanging shut of a metal door.
Scare, mistrust, and paranoia,
the start of another cold war.

Provideniya won't look at Nome,
Enurmino ignores Point Hope.
The Chukchi and the Bering wink.
The sea pulls off a rope-a-dope.

So the opportunity's gone
for the earth to impose its will.
The sea keeps the advantage
and is ready for the kill.

At the start of the fourteenth,
the earth moves on a different tack.
It knows it's just behind on points
and has to break Atlantic's back.

Donning a new appearance
and dominating the view,
it becomes that floating land mass
known as the *QM* 2.

On its maiden April voyage,
it leaves Southampton's port.
Rainy and grainy overhead,
like England's always taught.

Furrowing down the channel,
its whistle drowning the birds.
This piece of engineering
leaves passengers lost for words.

As it powers past Land's End
and heads for a distant shore,
the ocean sniggers to itself,
"You don't know what's in store."

And on the crossing's second day,
in water still and serene,
the ship's computer whizz girl
spots something odd upon her screen.

Transferring these vivid graphics
into her banks of data,
realizing what is out there
cannot be left till later.

Green eyes the size of heads
protrude from a wobbly skull.
His hideous arms by eight
are clamped around the hull.

His razor-serrated tongue—
a can opener with a lid—
his ink black sac a brewing,
it's the ferocious giant squid!

Over one hundred feet of flesh,
a bulging blue tumescence,
wreaking havoc down below
in an eerie phosphorescence.

And now he is unleashing
his oratory of fear,
scything through propellers,
making the ship change gear.

"Hard reverse," calls the commodore
to his Scottish first mate.
"Back up, and restart the engines
before it's too damned late."

Over the public address,
the captain calls for calm.
"Assemble at your stations.
There is no cause for alarm."

The diners in Todd's Restaurant
have *Titanic* on their minds.
"This isn't serendipity.
How could we have been so blind?"

But within an hour or so,
the glistening has died down.
The brutish monster underneath
has left this mid-sea town.

And Her Majesty sails on,
oblivious to danger.
Dreams of immortality,
a babe within a manger.

This vessel of class and breeding
steams on without a sail.
Doesn't catch the ocean murmur,
"What about a force 10 gale?"

And suddenly she shudders,
tossed around like balsa wood.
The sea is so enjoying this
as we always knew it would.

In the gilded state lecture room
tomes are put down for the day.
Themes of English literature
from the poem to the play.

The works of Geoffrey Chaucer,
Marlowe, Shakespeare, and John Donne.
Milton, Wordsworth, Keats, and Larkin,
and we've only just begun.

But literary giants
are not confined to land.
His years in the British merchant
helped Conrad's writing hand.

This is one of many pastimes
available on the trip
to our motley bunch of cruisers
from the doddery to the hip.

And back within their cabins,
the pilgrims are reflective.
The storm begins to weaken,
and they have a new perspective.

The entertainment director,
thinking, *Coulda, shoulda, oughta*,
instructs the resident band
to play something by Cole Porter.

The strings strike up a polka beat.
"Have you heard the coast of Maine,"
the, "Well, did you evah," song,
"Just Got Hit by a Hurricane."

What a *swelluva, helluva*
inappropriate number,
thinks Des, the bandleader,
anxious to play the set piece rumba.

But the players get sucked in.
"Every Time We Say Goodbye"
follows a yearning "Night and Day."
The babes pretend; the rich guys sigh.

So the band plays on regardless
into the Long Island ridge
as dawn climbs over Liberty
and the Verrazano Bridge.

The majestic liner docks,
massive and imperious.
The captain's manner calm,
his countenance somewhat serious.

He knows just how critical
was the penultimate round
to the teeming metropolites,
their concrete canyons bound.

The climax now awaits
with fourteen down and one to go.
Staggering from their stools,
each looking for a killer blow.

At the last and final round,
the fight is too close to call.
This is no time for saving strength;
they have to give it their all.

The sea girds its watery loins
and brings out the heavy guns.
Vast oceans of the world roll out,
a trillion liquid tons.

ROBERT W GREEN

The earth summons its resources
from all around the globe.
The Brazilian jungle limbers up;
Everest takes off his robe.

The rugged Grand Canyon,
the massive Canadian shield,
the Siberian steppes and tundra
declare, "We will never yield."

The Sahara Desert shimmers
in the searing noonday light.
Neither New York, London, nor Beijing
will surrender without a fight.

These and other great cities,
neoning through the night,
a mad kinetic energy
wound up explosively tight.

But the land is well outnumbered
by almost two to one.
The seas crash every coastline;
the earth refuses to run.

And so the round grinds on
with neither side backing down.
Ranging from the mightiest swells
to the tiniest seaside town.

An exhibition of courage
on every physical scale.
These elemental warriors
survive to tell the tale.

The timekeeper rings the final bell
as they collapse upon the floor.
The sky embraces both of them
and declares firmly, "It's a draw."

The audience goes mad,
clapping and stamping its feet.
The ref nods to the promoter,
who rises from his seat.

A host of network mics
are thrust into his face.
The Don holds up one hand
and says, "Next year, new place.

The public demands a rematch;
to me that's very clear.
I'll speak zeros to their managers
in deals they'll wanna hear."

The happy crowd disperses
back to the casino floor.
Arguing about the verdict,
agreeing they'd like some more.

Of course, life is one big crapshoot,
a turn of the card or wheel.
But the land, the sea, and the sky
are always part of the deal.

POSTSCRIPT

And so, as you all know,
that tough old land and pea-green sea
live together between bouts
in perfect harmony.

And wherever you are tonight,
the world is just one place.
So embrace all of its wonder,
and keep that smile upon your face.

TRAILER FOR THE REMATCH

Terms were agreed in the fall,
after wrangling over rights and place.
As a show of complete neutrality,
contracts were signed in outer space.

The Don was there of course.
His finished mop much whiter.
His grin was just as wide.
His wallet none the lighter.

Distribution was an issue
as it is for a major fight.
The parties agreed upon
cable, HBO, and satellite.

Ingram Content Group UK Ltd.
Milton Keynes UK
UKHW010119180523
421928UK00002B/12

9 781665 733380